Reading STREET

Grade 4

Pearson Scott Foresman
Leveled Reader
Teaching Guide

PEARSON

Glenview, Illinois • Boston, Massachusetts • Chandler, Arizona • Upper Saddle River, New Jersey

W9-BZO-944

Accelerated Reader®

ISBN: 13: 978-0-328-48449-2
ISBN: 10:   0-328-48449-0
3 4 5 6 7 8 9 10 V031 13 12 11 10

Table of Contents

Graphic Organizers

Introduction

Scott Foresman *Reading Street* provides more than 750 leveled readers that help students become better readers and build a lifelong love of reading. The *Reading Street* leveled readers are engaging texts that help students practice critical reading skills and strategies. They also provide opportunities to build vocabulary, understand concepts, and develop reading fluency.

The leveled readers were developed to be age-appropriate and appealing to students at each grade level. The leveled readers consist of engaging texts in a variety of genres, including fantasy, folk tales, realistic fiction, historical fiction, and narrative and expository nonfiction. To better address real-life reading skills that students will encounter in testing situations and beyond, a higher percentage of nonfiction texts is provided at each grade.

USING THE LEVELED READERS

You can use the leveled readers to meet the diverse needs of your students. Consider using the readers to

- practice critical skills and strategies
- build fluency
- build vocabulary and concepts
- build background for the main selections in the student book
- provide a variety of reading experiences, e.g., shared, group, individual, take-home, readers' theater

GUIDED READING APPROACH

The *Reading Street* leveled readers are leveled according to Guided Reading criteria by experts trained in Guided Reading. The Guided Reading levels increase in difficulty within a grade level and across grade levels. In addition to leveling according to Guided Reading criteria, the instruction provided in the *Leveled Reader Teaching Guide* is compatible with Guided Reading instruction. An instructional routine is provided for each leveled reader. This routine is most effective when working with individual students or small groups.

MANAGING THE CLASSROOM

When using the leveled readers with individuals or small groups, you'll want to keep the other students engaged in meaningful, independent learning tasks. Establishing independent practice stations throughout the classroom and routines for these stations can help you manage the rest of the class while you work with individuals or small groups. Practice stations can include listening, phonics, vocabulary, independent reading, and cross-curricular activities. For classroom management, create a work board that lists the stations and which students should be at each station. Provide instructions at each station that detail the tasks to be accomplished. Update the board and alert students when they should rotate to a new station. For additional support for managing your classroom, see the *Reading Street* Practice Stations' *Classroom Management Handbook*.

USING THE LEVELED READER TEACHING GUIDE

The *Leveled Reader Teaching Guide* provides an instruction plan for each leveled reader based on the same instructional routine.

INTRODUCE THE BOOK The Introduction includes suggestions for creating interest in the text by discussing the title and author, building background, and previewing the book and its features.

READ THE BOOK Before students begin reading the book, have them set purposes for reading and discuss how they can use the reading strategy as they read. Determine how you want students in a particular group to read the text, softly or silently, to a specific point or the entire text. Then use the Comprehension Questions to provide support as needed and to assess comprehension.

REVISIT THE BOOK The Reader Response questions provide opportunities for students to demonstrate their understanding of the text, the target comprehension skill, and vocabulary. The Response Options require students to revisit the text to respond to what they've read and to move beyond the text to explore related content.

SKILL WORK The Skill Work box provides instruction and practice for the target skill and strategy and selection vocabulary. Instruction for an alternate comprehension skill allows teachers to provide additional skill instruction and practice for students.

USING THE GRAPHIC ORGANIZERS

Graphic organizers in blackline-master format can be found on pages 132–152. These can be used as overhead transparencies or as student worksheets.

ASSESSING PERFORMANCE

Use the assessment forms that begin on page 6 to make notes about your students' reading skills, use of reading strategies, and general reading behaviors.

MEASURE FLUENT READING (pp. 6–7) Provides directions for measuring a student's fluency, based on words correct per minute (wcpm), and reading accuracy using a running record.

OBSERVATION CHECKLIST (p. 8) Allows you to note the regularity with which students demonstrate their understanding and use of reading skills and strategies.

STUDENT SELF-ASSESSMENT (p. 9) Helps students identify their own areas of strength and areas where they need further work. This form (About My Reading) encourages them to list steps they can take to become better readers and to set goals as readers. Suggest that students share their self-assessment notes with their families so that family members can work with them more effectively to practice their reading skills and strategies at home.

READING STRATEGY ASSESSMENT (p. 10) Provides criteria for evaluating each student's proficiency as a strategic reader.

PROGRESS REPORT (p. 11) Provides a means to track a student's book-reading progress over a period of time by noting the level at which a student reads and his or her accuracy at that level. Reading the chart from left to right gives you a visual model of how quickly a student is making the transition from one level to the next. Share these reports with parents or guardians to help them see how their child's reading is progressing.

Measure
Fluent Reading

Taking a Running Record

A running record is an assessment of a student's oral reading accuracy and oral reading fluency. Reading accuracy is based on the number of words read correctly. Reading fluency is based on the reading rate (the number of words correct per minute) and the degree to which a student reads with a "natural flow."

How to Measure Reading Accuracy

1. Choose a grade-level text of about 80 to 120 words that is unfamiliar to the student.
2. Make a copy of the text for yourself. Make a copy for the student or have the student read aloud from a book.
3. Give the student the text and have the student read aloud. (You may wish to record the student's reading for later evaluation.)
4. On your copy of the text, mark any miscues or errors the student makes while reading. See the running record sample on page 7, which shows how to identify and mark miscues.
5. Count the total number of words in the text and the total number of errors made by the student. Note: If a student makes the same error more than once, such as mispronouncing the same word multiple times, count it as one error. Self-corrections do not count as actual errors. Use the following formula to calculate the percentage score, or accuracy rate:

$$\frac{\text{Total Number of Words} - \text{Total Number of Errors}}{\text{Total Number of Words}} \times 100 = \text{percentage score}$$

Interpreting the Results

- A student who reads **95–100%** of the words correctly is reading at an **independent level** and may need more challenging text.
- A student who reads **90–94%** of the words correctly is reading at an **instructional level** and will likely benefit from guided instruction.
- A student who reads **89%** or fewer of the words correctly is reading at a **frustrational level** and may benefit most from targeted instruction with lower-level texts and intervention.

How to Measure Reading Rate (WCPM)

1. Follow Steps 1–3 above.
2. Note the exact times when the student begins and finishes reading.
3. Use the following formula to calculate the number of words correct per minute (WCPM):

$$\frac{\text{Total Number of Words Read Correctly}}{\text{Total Number of Seconds}} \times 60 = \text{words correct per minute}$$

Interpreting the Results

By the end of the year, a fourth-grader should be reading approximately 120–130 WCPM.

Running Record Sample

Running Record Sample

Notations

All the maple trees that grow in the   **8**

northeastern United States and parts of   **14**

Canada, have shaken off their slumber.   **20**

During the next few months, they put all *of*   **28**

their energy into growing. Maple trees   **34**

can live for hundreds of years. During   **41**

their first hundred years of existence,   **47**

they grow about ~~a~~ *one* foot each year.   **54**

The maple tree's roots anchor */an chor/*   **59**

the tree to the ground. They burrow   **66**

deep in the soil and push out in every   **75**

direction. The huge network of roots   **81**

(has) spread like an <u>enormous</u> *H* open hand   **88**

with dozens and dozens of outstretched   **94**

fingers in the ground. The deep roots   **101**

help keep the tree from toppling over   **108**

during strong winds. The roots also   **114**

gather nutrients (sc) the tree needs to   **120**

make sap.   **122**

Accurate Reading
The student reads a word correctly.

Insertion
The student inserts words or parts of words that are not in the text.

Substitution
The student substitutes words or parts of words for the words in the text.

Mispronunciation/Misreading
The student pronounces or reads a word incorrectly.

Omission
The student omits words or word parts.

Hesitation
The student hesitates over a word, and the teacher provides the word. Wait several seconds before telling the student what the word is.

Self-correction
The student reads a word incorrectly but then corrects the error. Do not count self-corrections as actual errors. However, noting self-corrections will help you identify words the student finds difficult.

Running Record Results
Total Number of Words: **122**
Number of Errors: **5**

Reading Time: **61 seconds**

▶ **Reading Accuracy**
$$\frac{122 - 5}{122} \times 100 = 95.902 = 96\%$$

Accuracy Percentage Score: **96%**

▶ **Reading Rate—WCPM**
$$\frac{117}{61} \times 60 = 115.08 = 115 \text{ words correct per minute}$$

Reading Rate: **115 WCPM**

Observation Checklist

Student's Name_____ Date_____

Behaviors Observed	Always (Proficient)	Usually (Fluent)	Sometimes (Developing)	Rarely (Novice)

Reading Strategies and Skills

Behaviors Observed	Always (Proficient)	Usually (Fluent)	Sometimes (Developing)	Rarely (Novice)
Uses prior knowledge and preview to understand what book is about				
Makes predictions and checks them while reading				
Uses context clues to figure out meanings of new words				
Uses phonics and syllabication to decode words				
Self-corrects while reading				
Reads at an appropriate reading rate				
Reads with appropriate intonation and stress				
Uses fix-up strategies				
Identifies story elements: character, setting, plot, theme				
Summarizes plot or main ideas accurately				
Uses target comprehension skill to understand the text better				
Responds thoughtfully about the text				

Reading Behaviors and Attitudes

	Always (Proficient)	Usually (Fluent)	Sometimes (Developing)	Rarely (Novice)
Enjoys listening to stories				
Chooses reading as a free-time activity				
Reads with sustained interest and attention				
Participates in discussion about books				

General Comments

About My Reading

Name _____ Date _____

1. **Compared with earlier in the year, I am enjoying reading**

   ☐ more   ☐ less   ☐ about the same

2. **When I read now, I understand**

   ☐ more than I used to   ☐ about the same as I used to

3. **One thing that has helped me with my reading is**

   _____

   _____

   _____

4. **One thing that could make me a better reader is**

   _____

   _____

   _____

5. **Here is one selection or book that I really enjoyed reading:**

   _____

   _____

6. **Here are some reasons why I liked it:**

   _____

   _____

   _____

   _____

   _____

Reading Strategy Assessment

Student _____ Date _____

Teacher _____

		Proficient	Developing	Emerging	Not showing trait
Building Background Comments:	Previews	☐	☐	☐	☐
	Asks questions	☐	☐	☐	☐
	Predicts	☐	☐	☐	☐
	Activates prior knowledge	☐	☐	☐	☐
	Sets own purposes for reading	☐	☐	☐	☐
	Other:	☐	☐	☐	☐
Comprehension Comments:	Retells/summarizes	☐	☐	☐	☐
	Questions, evaluates ideas	☐	☐	☐	☐
	Relates to self/other texts	☐	☐	☐	☐
	Paraphrases	☐	☐	☐	☐
	Rereads/reads ahead for meaning	☐	☐	☐	☐
	Visualizes	☐	☐	☐	☐
	Uses decoding strategies	☐	☐	☐	☐
	Uses vocabulary strategies	☐	☐	☐	☐
	Understands key ideas of a text	☐	☐	☐	☐
	Other:	☐	☐	☐	☐
Fluency Comments:	Adjusts reading rate	☐	☐	☐	☐
	Reads for accuracy	☐	☐	☐	☐
	Uses expression	☐	☐	☐	☐
	Other:	☐	☐	☐	☐
Connections Comments:	Relates text to self	☐	☐	☐	☐
	Relates text to text	☐	☐	☐	☐
	Relates text to world	☐	☐	☐	☐
	Other:	☐	☐	☐	☐
Self-Assessment Comments:	Is aware of: Strengths	☐	☐	☐	☐
	Needs	☐	☐	☐	☐
	Improvement/achievement	☐	☐	☐	☐
	Sets and implements learning goals	☐	☐	☐	☐
	Maintains logs, records, portfolio	☐	☐	☐	☐
	Works with others	☐	☐	☐	☐
	Shares ideas and materials	☐	☐	☐	☐
	Other:	☐	☐	☐	☐

Progress Report

Student's Name _____

At the top of the chart, record the book title, its grade/unit/week (for example, 1.2.3), and the student's accuracy percentage. See page 6 for measuring fluency, calculating accuracy and reading rates. At the bottom of the chart, record the date you took the running record. In the middle of the chart, make an X in the box across from the level of the student's reading— frustrational level (below 89% accuracy), instructional level (90–94% accuracy), or independent level (95–100% accuracy). Record the reading rate (WCPM) in the next row.

Book Title						
Grade/Unit/Week						
Reading Accuracy Percentage						
LEVEL Frustrational (89% or below)						
Instructional (90–94%)						
Independent (95% or above)						
Reading Rate (WCPM)						
Date						

Florida Everglades: Its Plants & Animals

SUMMARY This nonfiction book describes the special characteristics of many of the animals and plants native to the Florida Everglades. Some of the featured creatures include the black bear, alligator, mockingbird, and egret, as well as mangrove and cypress trees.

LESSON VOCABULARY

grand	memorial
peculiar	positive
prideful	recall
select	

INTRODUCE THE BOOK

INTRODUCE THE TITLE AND AUTHOR Discuss with students the title and the author of *Florida Everglades: Its Plants & Animals.* Point out the Social Studies content triangle on the cover, and then have students describe what sort of information they expect to learn about the Florida Everglades.

BUILD BACKGROUND Ask a student to locate the Everglades National Park on a map. Have students suggest what sort of climate the Everglades might have and why they think this. If any students have been to the Everglades, have them describe the types of plants and animals they saw there. If no one has been to the Everglades, have students guess what types of plants and animals might live in the park.

PREVIEW/USE TEXT FEATURES Have a student read the title of the book out loud. Then have other students skim through the book, looking at the pictures, captions, and headings. Discuss with students what types of plants and animals they will read about in the selection. Draw their attention to the circles appearing behind many of the pictures, and have students predict the reason the circles are there.

READ THE BOOK

SET PURPOSE Guide students to set their own purposes for reading the book, based on their predictions of the content. Write the following sentence on the board: I want to read this book to find out _____. Have students complete the sentence with their own purposes, based on what they would like to learn from the selection.

STRATEGY SUPPORT: SUMMARIZE Have students write down a summary sentence for each section, using the section heading as a guide. Give students an example for the first section by saying, "Some facts about bears are. . . ." Then fill in the rest of the sentence with one or two main ideas from the section.

COMPREHENSION QUESTIONS

PAGE 3 Draw a conclusion about the types of places black bears live in. *(Possible response: Black bears can live in many different kinds of places, such as warm or cold environments and wetland or upland forests.)*

PAGES 6–7 Summarize the types of food that black bears like to eat. *(plants and animals, insects, fruits, and nuts)*

PAGE 9 How does an alligator chase prey on land? *(It runs on its toes, lifts its tail off the ground, and sprints up to thirty miles an hour.)*

PAGE 11 What happened after many egrets were killed for their feathers? *(They became a protected species.)*

REVISIT THE BOOK

READER RESPONSE

1. Possible response: A bear might get hit by a car when it crosses a highway to get food and water.
2. Possible response: The mangrove tree can grow in salt water and its roots keep mud from being washed away. The cypress tree grows along the rivers and has "knees" that might help give it oxygen.
3. suffix: -ful; base word: pride. Other words: actually, dangerous, beautiful, luckily
4. Responses will vary but should be supported by details from the book.

EXTEND UNDERSTANDING Review with students their predictions about why some of the pictures in the book have circles drawn behind them. Discuss with students why these circles are in the pictures and what purpose they serve in helping the reader understand the information in the text.

RESPONSE OPTIONS

WRITING AND SPEAKING Have students write poems or songs about the plants or animals featured in *Florida Everglades: Its Plants & Animals,* using descriptions from the selection. Then have students present their poems and songs to the class.

SCIENCE CONNECTION

Provide students with a list of other plants and animals that live in Everglades National Park. Divide students into small groups. Assign one plant and one animal to each group. Have groups research their plants and animals and write short summaries of the facts they discover. Ask each group to read its summaries to the class.

Skill Work

TEACH/REVIEW VOCABULARY

Explain that a suffix may change the part of speech and meaning of a base word. Demonstrate that the root *pride* is a noun meaning "a high opinion of oneself." Adding *-ful* to the root makes *prideful*, which is an adjective meaning "having too high an opinion of oneself." Have students use a dictionary to find a new form of each vocabulary word using a suffix.

ELL Ask students to write the vocabulary words on index cards, with the definitions on the back. Have partners take turns picking cards from the pile. The student who picks a card acts out the word, and the partner tries to guess it.

TARGET SKILL AND STRATEGY

SEQUENCE Remind students that keeping track of the *sequence,* or order of events, in a book may help them understand the facts that are presented. Write a list of clue words on the chalkboard, such as *first, then, meanwhile,* and *now.* Tell students to look for these clue words as they read.

SUMMARIZE Tell students that *summarizing,* or remembering the important information in a book, can help them keep track of the sequence of events in a selection. Have students stop reading at the end of each section of the book and summarize the information in that section.

ADDITIONAL SKILL INSTRUCTION

DRAW CONCLUSIONS Review with students that a conclusion is a decision they reach that makes sense after they think about the facts and details presented in a book. Demonstrate that, for example, the picture on the cover of the book can lead the reader to draw the conclusion that the selection will contain information about some flowering plants and birds. Tell students that they should make decisions about the facts they read or the pictures they see in each section.

Sequence

- **Sequence** is the order of events.

Directions Use *Florida Everglades: Its Plants & Animals*. Answer the following questions.

1. What is the sequence of the information the author presents about black bears in the Florida Everglades?

_____

_____

2. Reread page 11. What sequence of events led to the protection of egrets?

First, _____

Next, _____

Now, _____

3. Reread page 14. What sequence of events led to the protection of the Florida Everglades?

First, _____

Next, _____

Now, _____

4. In what sequence does the selection tell about the plants and animals in the Florida Everglades?

First, _____

Next, _____

Next, _____

Next, _____

Finally, _____

Name _____

Vocabulary

Directions Use the vocabulary words in the box to fill in the blanks in the sentences below.

Check the Words You Know

___grand	___memorial	___peculiar	___positive
___prideful	___recall	___select	

1. I was _____ the black bear had not seen me.

2. Many people support putting up a _____ sign for all the black bears killed crossing highways.

3. Black bears like to _____ the tastiest berries.

4. Besides the armadillo, another _____ animal is the porcupine, with its unusual quills.

5. One of the most amazing habitats in North America is the _____ Florida Everglades.

6. Nina could not _____ where she had put her homework the night before.

7. People who live in Florida are _____ of many beautiful plants that grow in their state.

Directions Use a thesaurus to find antonyms for each of the words below.

8. grand _____

_____

9. peculiar _____

_____

10. prideful _____

_____

The Long Journey West

SUMMARY *The Long Journey West* tells the story of the expedition led by Meriwether Lewis and William Clark to map and explore the territory acquired during the Louisiana Purchase. The book describes some of the important events and people in the journey that took place between 1804 and 1806.

LESSON VOCABULARY

docks	migrating
scanned	scent
wharf	yearned

INTRODUCE THE BOOK

INTRODUCE THE TITLE AND AUTHOR Discuss with students the title and the author of *The Long Journey West*. Draw students' attention to the cover illustration, and have them describe what they can tell about the place and the people in the picture.

BUILD BACKGROUND Use a map to point out the western part of the United States, from the Mississippi River to the Pacific Ocean. Discuss with students what they know about the landscape and the history of the West. Ask students who have traveled in the West to talk about their trips.

PREVIEW/USE TEXT FEATURES Point out the maps in the text. Explain that the selection is about a journey into the American West at the time when the region had just become part of the United States. Then have students skim through the illustrations in the book. Have students predict what may have happened on this trip.

READ THE BOOK

SET PURPOSE Guide students to set their own purposes for reading the selection. Have them look through the pictures in the book again and choose one picture about which they would like to learn more. Tell students to use the pictures to create questions they would like to have answered, such as "What is the river that the people are traveling on?"

STRATEGY SUPPORT: QUESTIONING Remind students that asking good questions about important text information in a story is a good way to become a better reader. *Questioning* can take place before, during, or after reading a story. After previewing and setting a purpose for reading *The Long Journey West*, encourage students to ask themselves a question to keep in mind as they begin. Model: I wonder what this will be about.

COMPREHENSION QUESTIONS

PAGES 4–5 What did President Thomas Jefferson think would happen to the land from the Louisiana Purchase? *(Americans would begin migrating into the new territory.)*

PAGE 6 After reading this page, what do you think is the author's purpose for writing this book? *(to explain why Lewis and Clark made their trip through the American West)*

PAGES 10–11 Why was it important that the Corps got horses from the Shoshone and Salish? *(They needed the horses to cross the mountains.)*

PAGE 14 What question could you ask that would be answered by the information on this page? *(Possible response: When did Lewis and Clark and the Corps return to St. Louis?)*

REVISIT THE BOOK

READER RESPONSE

1. Possible response: He wanted to inform us about the Louisiana Purchase and Lewis and Clark's voyage with the Corps of Discovery.
2. Questions will vary, but make sure students are asking the questions from the point of view of Lewis or Clark.
3. Possible response: Scents in My Life: popcorn, bubble gum, shampoo, chocolate cake
   Scents on Lewis and Clark's Trip: smoke, fish, salt water
4. Possible response: The map shows the starting point and ending point of the trip.

EXTEND UNDERSTANDING Explain to students that authors of nonfiction texts often use headings as a way to organize the information they present. Discuss with students how the headings in the selection help achieve the author's purpose and contribute to readers' understanding of the topic.

RESPONSE OPTIONS

WRITING Have students imagine that they are members of the Lewis and Clark expedition. Tell them to choose one event from the selection and write a diary entry about it from the point of view of a member of the Corps of Discovery.

SCIENCE CONNECTION

Have each student use the Internet, an encyclopedia, or other resources to write a brief report about one of the plants or animals documented by Lewis and Clark.

Skill Work

TEACH/REVIEW VOCABULARY

Divide the class into six groups. Allot one vocabulary word to each group by having groups draw words from a box. Ask the groups to illustrate their words. Have groups present their illustrations while the rest of the class guesses the words.

TARGET SKILL AND STRATEGY

AUTHOR'S PURPOSE Review with students that authors have purposes, or reasons, for writing that are not always stated in the text. Point out that the reader can infer why the author wrote the book and that authors often have more than one reason for writing. Remind students that one common reason authors write nonfiction is to inform. Based on the genre and topic, have students discuss why they think the author might have written this book.

QUESTIONING Have students revisit and answer the questions they asked themselves before they began to read *The Long Journey West*. Then have them generate a final question such as *I wonder what the author wanted me to remember from this story*.

ADDITIONAL SKILL INSTRUCTION

MAIN IDEA AND DETAILS Review with students that the *main idea* is the most important idea about a topic. Supporting *details* are small pieces of information about the main idea. As students read, have them look for the main idea about the topic, Lewis and Clark's long trip West. When they have finished reading the selection, have students write the main idea in a sentence. Then tell them to go back to the text to find three supporting details.

ELL Have students use a Main Idea and Details graphic organizer and write key words in each section of the organizer.

Author's Purpose

- The **author's purpose** is the reason or reasons an author has for writing. For example, the author may want *to inform, persuade, entertain,* or *express* a mood or feeling.
- An author may have one or more reason for writing.

Directions Read the following passage from *The Long Journey West*. Think about the author's purposes as you read. Then, for each question below, circle the letter of the best answer.

On May 26, 1805, Lewis scanned the horizon. He saw the Rocky Mountains for the first time. They were rugged and tall. The Corps of Discovery traded with Sacagawea's Shoshone and with another Native American nation, the Salish. They got horses to ride through the mountains.

The trip over the steep mountains was tough. The weather was very cold. It was hard to find food. Many of the men were starving.

But the Corps of Discovery kept going. They made it over the mountains. Now they had to cross rivers. They left the horses behind and made canoes. The Corps of Discovery yearned to see the Pacific Ocean. In November of 1805 the Corps of Discovery finally reached the ocean.

1. The genre of this passage is
   a. science fiction.   b. poetry.   c. fiction.   d. nonfiction.

2. What do you think is the author's main purpose for writing this passage?
   a. to inform   b. to persuade   c. to express   d. to entertain

3. What do you think was the author's purpose for describing the trip over the mountains in the second paragraph?
   a. to persuade the reader that people should not ride horses
   b. to inform the reader about what the Rocky Mountains are like in the summer
   c. to entertain by making the reader feel fearful and worried about the Corps
   d. to express the feeling of joy that the men felt as they climbed the mountains

4. How do you think the author probably wants the reader to feel at the end of this passage?
   a. distrustful   b. sad   c. nervous   d. happy

Vocabulary

Directions Choose the word from the box that best matches each definition. Write the word on the line. Use each word only once.

Check the Words You Know

___docks	___migrating	___scanned
___scent	___wharf	___yearned

1. _____ wharfs

2. _____ moving from one region to another

3. _____ to glance at; look over hastily

4. _____ felt a longing or desire; desired earnestly

5. _____ a platform built on the shore or out from the shore beside which ships can load and unload

6. _____ a smell

Directions Sort the words according to the description in each box.

Nouns

7. _____

8. _____

9. _____

Words with Endings

10. _____

11. _____

12. _____

13. _____

From Sea to Shining Sea

◎ **CHARACTER, SETTING, AND PLOT**
◎ **BACKGROUND KNOWLEDGE**

SUMMARY This fictional journal chronicles the journey of a group of explorers, led by Merriwether Lewis and William Clark, who are sent by President Thomas Jefferson to explore the West. They are asked to find rivers and oceans that can be used as a means of transporting trade goods, collect new plants and animals, make friends with native tribes, and study rocks along the trail. This journal is written from the perspective of Tad, one of the members in the group.

LESSON VOCABULARY

badger	bank	bristled
jointed	patched	ruffled
rushes		

INTRODUCE THE BOOK

INTRODUCE THE TITLE AND AUTHOR Discuss the title and author of *From Sea to Shining Sea*. Have students describe what they see in the cover illustration. Ask students what they think the boy is writing about and how it may relate to the title of the story.

BUILD BACKGROUND Ask students if they have explored a new place before. Have students share their experiences. Discuss journaling and how it is one way to describe the people, surroundings, and events at a new place. Discuss how the land that makes up the United States was explored over time and that new discoveries were often shared through writing.

PREVIEW/USE TEXT FEATURES Have students look at the illustrations on the pages of the book. After students have previewed the book, discuss the text feature of a date at the top of each text section. Ask: What did you notice about the dates from page to page? *(skipping over a period of 3 years)* Why do you think it took so long?

READ THE BOOK

SET PURPOSE Have students set a purpose for reading *From Sea to Shining Sea*. Have students think about a time when they went somewhere new. Ask: Who was there? What would you write to describe the new place? What happened? How long did it take you to get there?

STRATEGY SUPPORT: BACKGROUND KNOWLEDGE EHave students write what they already know about the western part of the United States. As they read and gather more information about the West, have them add to their "know" list.

COMPREHENSION QUESTIONS

PAGES 4–5 Why did President Jefferson send these explorers West? *(To look for rivers and oceans for transportation of goods, to find new plants and animals, meet different native people, and study rocks along their travels.)*

PAGE 10 What types of places or settings have the explorers been to and where are they now? *(Rivers, plains, tribe reservation, fort and now the mountains.)*

PAGE 13 How are the explorers feeling? Why? *(Joyful; because they have reached their goal of finding the ocean.)*

PAGE 15 How long did it take the explorers to go West and return home? How do you know? *(3 years; because the journal dates started in August 1803 and ended fall 1806.)*

REVISIT THE BOOK

READER RESPONSE

1. Lewis, Clark, Corps of Discovery, Sacagawea, Tad, President Thomas Jefferson; rivers, plains, tribe reservation, fort, mountains, Pacific Ocean
2. Responses will vary but make sure students include what they understood from previewing the illustrations in the book.
3. Possible responses: a place to keep money; the land on the side of a river, lake or ocean.
4. Responses will vary but make sure students understand the time period and what would have been available to them at that time.

EXTEND UNDERSTANDING Have students look at the map on page 13. Explain the symbols for the topographical features on the map and discuss the different types of terrain this group explored. Visually trace and discuss the trail the explorers followed from St. Louis to the Pacific. Make connections with the descriptions Tad wrote about for these settings.

RESPONSE OPTIONS

WRITING Have students write a journal entry about a time when they explored a new place (this can be real or fiction). Remind students to include the people (characters), surroundings (setting), and what happened (plot) during this exploration. Have students include dates or times in sequence. Students may include illustrations to support their descriptions.

SOCIAL STUDIES CONNECTION

Time For **SOCIAL STUDIES**

Have students research factual information about Lewis and Clark's exploration. Have them record the information in sequence of the exploration and discoveries.

ELL Have students who are new to the United States research an explorer from their native country.

Skill Work

TEACH/REVIEW VOCABULARY

From page 5, write on the board: *Today I found a badger. It is an animal that weighs about 13 pounds.* Help students use context clues to define the vocabulary word badger. *(an animal that weighs about 13 pounds)* In partners, have students find the remaining vocabulary words and define each word using context clues from the story.

TARGET SKILL AND STRATEGY

CHARACTER, SETTING, AND PLOT Remind students that *characters* are the people or animals who participate in the events of a story. The *setting* is the time and place in which a story takes place. A story's *plot* is the most important events in the story, including the problem or conflict, the rising action, the climax, and the solution or outcome/resolution. As students read, have them ask themselves: Who are the main characters? Where have they traveled? What are the most important events in this story?

BACKGROUND KNOWLEDGE Explain to students that *background knowledge* is information that they already know about a topic. Point out that making connections to what they already know can help them understand a story's plot. Discuss with students what they already know about Lewis and Clark's explorations, the western part of the United States, and journals.

ADDITIONAL SKILL INSTRUCTION

DRAW CONCLUSIONS Remind students that *sequence* is the term for the order of events in a story. Review the order of journal entry dates for time sequence. Have students create a timeline and mark the dates accordingly.

Character, Setting, and Plot

- A **character** in a story is a person or animal that takes part in the events of the story.
- The **setting** is the time and place in which a story occurs.
- The **plot** is the important events, usually organized around a problem or conflict.

Directions Use information from *From Sea to Shining Sea* to complete the sentences below.

This story is about _____

_____

This story takes place (name the characters) _____

_____

The action begins when (where and when) _____

_____

_____

Then, _____

_____

_____

Next, _____

_____

_____

After that, _____

_____

_____

The story ends when _____

_____

_____

Vocabulary

Directions Unscramble each vocabulary word and write it correctly on the line. Write a sentence using each vocabulary word.

Check the Words You Know

___ badger	___ rushes	___ patched	___ ruffled
___ jointed	___ bank	___ bristled	

1. frelduf _____

    Your Sentence: _____

2. garbed _____

    Your Sentence: _____

3. shesru _____

    Your Sentence: _____

4. kbna _____

    Your Sentence: _____

5. dntoeij _____

    Your Sentence: _____

6. dtblries _____

    Your Sentence: _____

7. thepadc _____

    Your Sentence: _____

Flash Flood

SUMMARY In this fiction book, Jimmy and his parents set out on a camping trip in North Dakota. Along the way, a heavy rain begins to fall. The river along which they are traveling rises dangerously high, so Jimmy and his parents abandon their camper to flee a flash flood. Will the camper be washed away? Will Jimmy and his parents be safe from the flood?

LESSON VOCABULARY

bargain	favors	lassoed
offended	prairie	riverbed
shrieked		

INTRODUCE THE BOOK

INTRODUCE THE TITLE AND AUTHOR Discuss with students the title and the author of *Flash Flood*. Use a word web on the board and brainstorm with students all the words that come to mind when they think of the term *flash flood.*

ELL Have students share the words that mean "flood" in their home languages and discuss with them whether they have terms for *flash flood.*

BUILD BACKGROUND Ask students if any of them have ever been involved in a flood. Have volunteers describe the situation, such as where they were when the flood happened and what they did to remain safe. Tell students that sometimes heavy rains can cause rivers and other waterways to overflow in a short amount of time, a phenomenon known as a flash flood.

PREVIEW/USE TEXT FEATURES Have students skim through the book, looking at the pictures. Ask: What do you think this story is about? What do you think the story will be like—happy, sad, funny, scary, or something else? What gives you that idea?

READ THE BOOK

SET PURPOSE Have students complete the following sentence with their own purposes: *I want to read this book because _____.* Suggest that they might read a fictional story because they want to be entertained, to feel a certain mood, or to learn about something new.

STRATEGY SUPPORT: STORY STRUCTURE Draw a story structure diagram on the board, shaped like an inverted *V*. Label the diagram: *Conflict* at the bottom of the left-hand prong; *Rising Action* along the left prong; *Climax* at the peak; *Falling Action* along the right prong; and *Resolution* at the bottom of the right-hand prong. Have students copy the diagram into their notebooks. As they read, suggest that they write down the events in the story that fit each part of the diagram.

COMPREHENSION QUESTIONS

PAGES 6-7 What were Jimmy and his parents worried about? *(They were worried that there would be a flash flood and that the river would wash out the road.)*

PAGES 9-11 How do you think the author wants you to feel at this point in the story? How do you know this? *(Possible response: She wants us to feel scared and anxious. We know this because she uses words like* yelled, scared, gulped, *and* quickly. *The pictures also show the danger of the situation.)*

PAGE 12 What do you think is the author's purpose in describing how Jimmy felt and how his parents acted? *(Possible response: She wants to create a mood of fear and excitement. She also wants to create rising action toward the climax.)*

PAGES 14-15 Summarize the resolution, or the end of the story. *(Possible response: Jimmy and his parents remained safe from the flood because they left their camper behind and moved to higher ground.)*

REVISIT THE BOOK

READER RESPONSE

1. Possible response: The author wrote *Flash Flood* to entertain and give information about flash floods and how they happen.
2. Possible response: Beginning—Jimmy's family leaves for vacation; Middle—a storm causes dangerous flooding; End—Jimmy's family moves to higher ground until the storm ends.
3. deal
4. Possible response: move quickly to higher ground; scared or worried

EXTEND UNDERSTANDING Point out that authors use adjectives to help readers create mental pictures of the characters, setting, and events in a story. Explain that authors choose their adjectives depending on what purpose they have for writing the story. For example, a writer might describe a house as *dark, empty, cold, and spooky* to create a mood of fear and anticipation in the reader. Have students review the book and find three adjectives that helped them create mental pictures. Discuss how these mental pictures served the author's purpose.

RESPONSE OPTIONS

SPEAKING Have students act out parts of the story using the dialogue in the book. Remind them that when they play their parts, they should use tones of voice that reflect the mood and action in the story.

SCIENCE CONNECTION

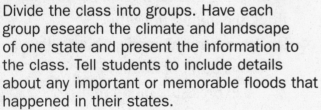

On a map, locate the prairie states, also known as the Great Plains, for the class. Divide the class into groups. Have each group research the climate and landscape of one state and present the information to the class. Tell students to include details about any important or memorable floods that happened in their states.

Skill Work

TEACH/REVIEW VOCABULARY

Write the vocabulary words on the board. Divide the class into seven groups and assign one word to each group. Have each group find its word in the selection and define the word using context clues. Ask each group to share its definition with the class.

TARGET SKILL AND STRATEGY

AUTHOR'S PURPOSE Remind students that authors have reasons for writing stories—to persuade, inform, entertain, or express a mood or feeling. Tell students that an author often has more than one purpose. Ask students to keep in mind the predictions they made during the Preview part of the lesson. Have them consider, while they read, whether their predictions about the author's purpose were correct.

STORY STRUCTURE Review with students the four parts of *story structure:* conflict (or problem), rising action, climax, and resolution (or outcome). Remind students that a conflict may be between characters, between characters and nature, or within a character. Discuss with students how the story structure in fiction can help the author entertain, create a mood or feeling, or even inform or persuade. Invite students to look for these parts of the story structure as they read.

ADDITIONAL SKILL INSTRUCTION

MAIN IDEA AND DETAILS Review with students that the *main idea* of a fictional story is what the story is all about. Remind students that they should be able to tell the main idea of *Flash Flood* in just one or two sentences. Also review with students that supporting *details* are the small pieces of information that tell more about the main idea. Once students have come up with a main idea for the story, have them go back and skim the book to find three or four details that support the main idea.

Name _____

Author's Purpose

- The **author's purpose** is the reason or reasons an author has for writing.
- An author may have one or more reasons for writing. He or she may want *to inform, persuade, entertain,* or *express* a mood or feeling.

Directions Read the following passage. Then answer the questions below.

Jimmy kept watching the river. The whipping wind shrieked outside the camper. Jimmy felt more and more nervous.

"The dry ground of these riverbeds can become almost as hard as rocks. When it rains, the hardened riverbed cannot absorb all the water," the radio announcer said.

"Riverbeds can overflow during rain storms, flooding roads and houses. It happens really fast. That's why they are called flash floods. Drivers beware: In a flood, it takes only two feet of water to wash away a car."

Jimmy pictured rushing water overflowing a dry riverbed as he stared out the window.

1. This text is
   a. fiction.
   b. nonfiction.
   c. poetry.
   d. drama.

2. The author's main purpose for writing this passage was probably to
   a. show the importance of radio announcers.
   b. explain how campers can float.
   c. entertain the reader by making the reader feel scared and nervous.
   d. express a feeling of calm by describing the wind and rain.

3. Another purpose the author may have had for writing this passage was to
   a. tell the reader that people should not worry about flash floods.
   b. express Jimmy's feeling of anger that he and his family were riding in a camper.

   c. entertain the reader by describing the fun and excitement Jimmy was having as he watched the river rise.
   d. inform the reader about what causes flash floods and how dangerous they are.

4. The author writes the passage from the point of view of the boy, Jimmy, so that the reader knows what Jimmy is thinking and feeling. Why do you think the author does this?
   a. to inform the reader about what boys think of adults
   b. to express the mood of nervousness that Jimmy was feeling
   c. to persuade the reader that Jimmy knows a lot about campers
   d. to entertain the reader by making fun of Jimmy

Vocabulary

Directions Match the words in column A with their synonyms in column B.

Check the Words You Know

___bargain   ___favors   ___lassoed   ___offended
___prairie   ___riverbed   ___shrieked

Column A

1. lassoed

2. shrieked

3. offended

4. bargain

5. favors

6. prairie

Column B

a. good deal

b. good deeds

c. roped

d. upset

e. cried out

f. flat grassland

Directions Write a brief story or poem about a cowboy or cowgirl using the words *prairie*, *riverbed*, and *lassoed*.

_____

_____

_____

_____

_____

_____

_____

_____

_____

America's National Parks

SUMMARY This nonfiction book introduces students to some of the important natural and historical parks in the United States.

LESSON VOCABULARY

glaciers	impressive	naturalists
preserve	slopes	species
wilderness		

INTRODUCE THE BOOK

INTRODUCE THE TITLE AND AUTHOR Discuss with students the title and the author of *America's National Parks*. Use a concept web on the board for the word *parks*, and brainstorm with students related ideas and words. Have students discuss which ideas might be topics of this book, based on the cover picture and genre.

BUILD BACKGROUND Tell students that the "park" discussed in this book is our national parkland. Locate some of the important parks in the selection on a map, such as Yellowstone and Denali National Parks, the Grand Canyon, and Colonial National Historical Park. Discuss what students know about these places. Have students who have been to any of these parks talk about their visits there.

PREVIEW/USE TEXT FEATURES Have students look through the book. Draw their attention to the pictures, captions, headings, and the time line. Ask: Why are there headings in this book? *(to group facts together by topic, to help the reader follow the information)* Besides the text, what other ways does the author present information? *(pictures and captions, a time line)*

READ THE BOOK

SET PURPOSE Invite students to think about one question they might have about America's national parks. Have students use their questions as their purpose for reading and finding answers in the text.

STRATEGY SUPPORT: TEXT STRUCTURE As students read, point out the internal text structure of the book. Have students turn to page 3 and identify the heading. *(Our National Parks)* Remind students that headings help organize a book into sections. In this section, students will be reading about national parks.

ELL To ensure comprehension of the text by speakers of other languages, have students use the Main Idea and Details graphic organizer to chart the information in subsections of the text.

COMPREHENSION QUESTIONS

PAGES 4–5 What generalization could you make from the information on these pages? *(Possible response: Many Americans wanted to protect the natural wonders in America.)*

PAGES 6–7 What is the main idea on these two pages? *(Some national parks were set up to protect important historical places.)*

PAGES 8–9 Why do plants and animals in Denali National Park have to be tough? *(Most of the ground stays frozen, and the winters are long and harsh.)*

PAGES 10–11 The main idea of this section is "Colonial National Historical Park allows visitors to see what life was like in America for the first English settlers." What are some supporting details for this main idea? *(Possible responses: Old Towne preserves the site of the first English settlement, guides wear clothes like the first settlers, visitors can learn about the life of Pocahontas.)*

PAGE 13 What is the job of the National Park Service? *(to manage our national parks)*

REVISIT THE BOOK

READER RESPONSE

1. Possible responses: Main idea: Our national parks preserve nature and history. Supporting details: Mesa Verde National Park preserves the cliff dwellings of the ancestral Pueblo people; Colonial National Historical Park preserves the site of the first English settlement; Denali National Park protects mountains, plants, and animals in Alaska.
2. Responses will vary, but should include the headings "Our National Parks," "Historical Sites," "Landscapes and Wildlife," "Another Historical Park," and "Preserving Wildlife."
3. impressive, naturalist. Possible responses: The mountain was impressive. My uncle is a naturalist.
4. Possible response: when some state and national parks were founded

EXTEND UNDERSTANDING

Point out that headings in nonfiction organize the facts in a text into groups. Headings also may help the reader understand the main ideas presented in a selection. Discuss with students how the headings in *America's National Parks* help them understand the main ideas and supporting details of the book.

RESPONSE OPTIONS

WRITING Have students use their Main Idea and Details graphic organizers to write paragraphs summarizing the selection.

SOCIAL STUDIES CONNECTION

Time For SOCIAL STUDIES

Have each student choose a park featured in the selection. Tell each student to find out more about his or her park using books or the Internet and to write a paragraph describing one special feature there. Have students present their special places to the class.

Skill Work

TEACH/REVIEW VOCABULARY

Read through the Glossary with the class. Have groups of students locate the words in the selection and write their own sentences for the words. Share the sentences as a class.

TARGET SKILL AND STRATEGY

MAIN IDEA AND DETAILS Remind students that a topic is what a selection is about, while the *main idea* is the most important idea about the topic. Supporting *details* are small pieces of information that tell more about the main idea. Ask: What is the topic of this book? *(U.S. national parks)* Discuss with students that the main idea will be the most important idea in the book about national parks. Have them look for the main idea as they read.

TEXT STRUCTURE Review with students that *text structure* is how the book is organized. Ask questions to test students' understanding of text structure, such as: If I wanted to quickly find a section that talks about animals in this book, what headings would it most likely be under? *(Landscapes and Wildlife, Preserving Wildlife)*

ADDITIONAL SKILL INSTRUCTION

GENERALIZE Remind students that sometimes when they read, they can make statements that apply to several ideas, things, or people in a text. This statement is called a *generalization.* Explain that a generalization may be about how items are mostly or all alike. As an example, make a generalization about birds: All birds have feathers. Point out words that may signal generalizations, such as *all*, *most*, *many*, *usually*, and *generally*. As they read, have students think of a generalization that applies to some ideas or items in the text.

Main Idea and Details

- The **main idea** is the most important idea about the topic of a paragraph, passage, or article.

- Supporting **details** are the small pieces of information that tell more about the main idea.

Directions Read the following passage. Then tell the main idea of the passage and list the supporting details that tell more about the main idea.

Grand Canyon National Park is one of the most famous parks in the world. Scientists come from many countries to study the Canyon. They are interested in the Canyon's landscape. The Canyon was made millions of years ago. Its steep cliffs still hold fossils and rocks from times long gone. The Canyon is also home to many types of plants and animals. Many scientists visit the Canyon to study its wildlife. Of course, many tourists also travel to the Canyon just to admire its beauty.

Topic: Grand Canyon National Park

↓

Main Idea

1.

↓

Supporting Details

2.

3.

4.

Vocabulary

Directions Match the word from Column A with its definition in Column B.
Write the letter of the correct definition next to each word in Column A.

Check the Words You Know

___glaciers   ___impressive   ___naturalists   ___preserve
___slopes   ___species   ___wilderness

Column A

_____ 1. naturalists

_____ 2. slopes

_____ 3. wilderness

_____ 4. glaciers

_____ 5. preserve

Column B

a. great masses of ice moving very slowly down mountains, along valleys, or over land areas

b. people who study living things

c. a wild, uncultivated region with few or no people living in it

d. to keep from harm or change; keep safe; protect

e. lines, surfaces, land, or other objects that go up or down at an angle

Directions Choose the word from the box that best completes each sentence.
Write the word on the line.

6. Mt. McKinley in Alaska is the most _____ mountain in America.

7. There are many different _____ of plants and animals living in Yosemite National Park.

8. It is important to have national parks to _____ our most beautiful places.

9. The skier did not expect to find such steep _____.

10. People who hike in the _____ need to take along a map and plenty of water.

Cheers for the Cheetahs

SUMMARY This is a fictional story about a group of girls trying to convince the male coach at their school that they can play basketball as well as the boys. The story is about equality and standing up for your rights to receive equal and fair treatment. It's also a story about using your strengths, which is shown when Hannah, one of the less-talented players, is chosen to write a letter of concern to the principal.

LESSON VOCABULARY

fouled	hoop
jersey	marveled
rim	speechless
swatted	unbelievable

INTRODUCE THE BOOK

INTRODUCE THE TITLE AND AUTHOR Discuss with students the title and the author of *Cheers for the Cheetahs*. Based on the title and the illustration on the cover, ask students to describe what they think this book may be about. Ask students why they think the cover illustration pictures girls from different ethnic backgrounds.

BUILD BACKGROUND Ask students to talk about instances when they or someone they know has been treated unfairly. Discuss what they or the other person did about the situation.

PREVIEW/USE TEXT FEATURES After students have previewed the book, discuss what they think the story is about based on the illustrations. Ask: Who are the Cheetahs?

READ THE BOOK

SET PURPOSE Have students set a purpose for reading *Cheers for the Cheetahs*. Students' interest in sports and in how boys and girls may be treated differently could guide this purpose. Suggest that students think about how standing up for themselves can help them in any experience in life.

STRATEGY SUPPORT: PRIOR KNOWLEDGE As students read about the girls' efforts to be able to play basketball, remind them to refer to what they know about this topic. Suggest that they write two sentences about an unfair situation. Help them understand that by using their own knowledge, they can see the causes and effects of the problem more easily. Also remind students that when causes are not clearly stated in the text, reflecting on their own experience may help them identify causes and effects.

COMPREHENSION QUESTIONS

PAGE 6 What did Hannah and Goldie want to prove? *(that the girls in their fourth-grade class could play basketball as well as any of the boys)*

PAGE 10 Why was writing a letter a risk? *(The principal or Mr. Giddings could get mad.)*

PAGE 11 Was Mr. Giddings deliberately ignoring the girls? How do you know? *(No, he was speechless when he was told they were upset.)*

PAGE 15 When Mr. Giddings saw the girls play, what effect did that have on him? *(He realized how talented they were and asked them to be on a co-ed team.)*

REVISIT THE BOOK

READER RESPONSE

1. Possible responses: Causes: The gym teacher wouldn't give the girls a chance; the girls felt they weren't treated equally; the girls thought they were just as good as the boys. Effects: The girls formed a team with jerseys; the girls played the boys and won; the girls won the gym teacher's respect.
2. Possible responses: I know that playing sports takes teamwork or that anyone can be a great player if you give that person a chance.
3. *Un-* means "not" or "opposite of." *Unbelievable* means "not believable; incredible." Students should list at least two additional words with the prefix *un-*.
4. Responses will vary, but they should include a reasonable explanation.

EXTEND UNDERSTANDING Remind students that characters are the people whom a story is about. Draw attention to Hannah's actions in the story. Hannah is not the best athlete in the story, but she scores very important points for the team because she writes a letter. Guide students in a discussion about why this letter is so important for the team and so important for Hannah.

RESPONSE OPTIONS

WRITING To explore how silly some stereotypes can be, invite students to write a commentary about why cats are much smarter, faster, and better than dogs and why no dogs should be allowed in the country. Have students read their commentaries to the class.

SPORTS CONNECTION

Have students identify and research famous female athletes. Have volunteers present their findings to the class.

Skill Work

TEACH/REVIEW VOCABULARY

Use each vocabulary word in a sentence. Have students use that context to determine the meaning of the word and what part of speech it is.

ELL Have students make a flashcard for each vocabulary word. Guide them to write the word on one side of the card and the definition on the other. Then have them work in pairs to quiz each other on the words using the flashcards.

TARGET SKILL AND STRATEGY

CAUSE AND EFFECT Remind students that *cause* refers to why something happens and *effect* refers to what happens as a result of that cause. Give students a few sentences that present examples of cause and effect. Have them identify the causes and the effects.

PRIOR KNOWLEDGE Remind students that *prior knowledge* is the information about a subject that they already know. Ask students to discuss what they already know about the difference between boys' and girls' sports teams.

ADDITIONAL SKILL INSTRUCTION

PLOT Remind students that the *plot* of a story has to do with the events that make up the story. Plot is what the story is about. A plot has a beginning (which sets up the problem), a middle (which details what is done about the problem), and an ending (which usually provides a solution to the problem). As students read, suggest that they take notes on what they think is the beginning, the middle, and the end of the story.

Cause and Effect

- A **cause** is *why* something happens. An **effect** is *what* happens.
- Sometimes there is more than one cause of an effect, and sometimes there are multiple effects of a cause.

Directions Answer the questions on the lines provided.

1. Why did Mr. Giddings give the boys more gym time? What was the cause of his actions?

   _____

   _____

2. Although Hannah was not the best player, she did something important for the team that no one else could do. What was this?

   _____

   _____

3. What did Hannah and her teammates risk by speaking out for themselves? What was the benefit of speaking out?

   _____

   _____

4. Based on what you know after having read the story, how do you think the coach will act differently from now on? Why?

   _____

   _____

5. What lesson do you think this story teaches about standing up for yourself?

   _____

   _____

Name _____

Vocabulary

Directions Draw a line from the vocabulary word to its correct definition.

Check the Words You Know

___fouled   ___hoop   ___jersey

___marveled   ___rim   ___speechless

___swatted   ___unbelievable

1. swatted

2. fouled

3. hoop

4. jersey

5. marveled

6. rim

7. speechless

8. unbelievable

a. not able to be believed

b. made an error in the game

c. wondered

d. a ring; a round, flat band

e. the edge

f. unable to speak

g. a shirt

h. hit sharply or violently

Directions Unscramble the vocabulary words and then write a definition for each one.

9. ludefo _____

Definition:_____

10. poho _____

Definition:_____

11. yjrese _____

Definition:_____

12. mir _____

Definition:_____

13. eulvalenebib _____

Definition:_____

35

Ranches in the Southwest

SUMMARY This book explores ranch life in the Southwest. Students will learn about the changes that have happened in ranch life, including how ranchers began inviting guests to ensure the ranches wouldn't go out of business and how this benefited both the guests and the ranchers.

LESSON VOCABULARY

bawling	coyote
dudes	roundup
spurs	

INTRODUCE THE BOOK

INTRODUCE THE TITLE AND AUTHOR Discuss with students the title and the author of *Ranches in the Southwest.* Ask students to share what they know about ranch life and about the southwestern region of the United States. Direct students' attention to the photograph on the cover and ask them what they think is going on in the picture.

BUILD BACKGROUND Ask students if they have ever gone to a ranch or seen cowboy movies that take place on ranches. Based on their impressions, ask students what other information they think they might learn from the book.

PREVIEW/USE TEXT FEATURES Suggest that students look through the book and study the photographs and chapter titles. Ask students what information the photographs and titles give them about life on a ranch.

READ THE BOOK

SET PURPOSE Have students set a purpose for reading *Ranches in the Southwest.* Students' interest in the West and in dude ranches should help guide this purpose.

STRATEGY SUPPORT: TEXT STRUCTURE As students read, model how to identify the internal text structure of a book. Remind students that they took note of the book's chapter titles in their preview. Lead them to see how the chapter titles can help them understand how the author organized the book.

COMPREHENSION QUESTIONS

PAGE 5 Based on what you read about ranchers' problems, why are dude ranches a good idea? *(They provide income for the ranchers.)*

PAGE 6 How does the poster help you understand why people might want to go to a dude ranch? *(Possible response: The word* glamour *makes the idea of going to a ranch sound exciting and interesting.)*

PAGES 8–9 What conclusions can you draw about the kind of experience guests on a ranch want? *(Possible response: Lodging is simple but comfortable. It is not really roughing it. At the same time, guests come to work.)*

PAGE 11 How is life for a rancher different from life for a guest on a ranch? *(Ranchers and their families live there year-round; in winter they work from dawn until eight at night.)*

PAGE 14 What conclusion can you draw about what is needed from ranchhands as they rope and brand calves? *(cooperation)*

REVISIT THE BOOK

READER RESPONSE

1. Possible responses might mention that ranching damages the environment. Some ranchers might move their cattle more often to limit damage from overgrazing.

2. Possible response: The chapter titles tell me what that part of the book will be about. Students' lists will vary, but titles should be spelled correctly and each list should have two items indicating what students learned from that section.

3. Possible responses: Definition One: to feed on grass and other plants, usually in a meadow. Definition Two: to brush lightly.

4. Sights: branding, roping, separating of calves from their mothers; Sounds: bawling calves, lowing cows, guests roping.

EXTEND UNDERSTANDING Have students brainstorm how a ranch is different than a farm. Encourage students to think about the purpose of a ranch as opposed to that of a farm. Have them think of the kinds of plant and animals they might find on each. List their ideas on the board.

RESPONSE OPTIONS

WRITING Suggest that students imagine they are guests on a dude ranch and ask them to write letters home telling about their time on the ranch.

SOCIAL STUDIES CONNECTION

Time For SOCIAL STUDIES

Invite students to do more research on ranch life. Then have them work as a class to make a ranch scrapbook. Students can put in campfire recipes, camp songs, and "to do" lists of ranch chores.

Skill Work

TEACH/REVIEW VOCABULARY

Review vocabulary with students. Then ask students to write short paragraphs about any topics they choose, using all of the vocabulary words.

ELL Review vocabulary words with students. Ask: If I saw a bawling calf, what would the calf be doing? Do the same with all vocabulary words.

TARGET SKILL AND STRATEGY

DRAW CONCLUSIONS Remind students that *drawing a conclusion* means arriving at a decision or opinion that make sense after thinking about some facts and details. Give students a list of facts about parrots: *Parrots can learn to speak. Parrots pine for their mates. Parrots can learn tricks.* Ask students what conclusion they can draw from these facts. *(Parrots are smart.)* Then suggest that students write down facts as they read *Ranches in the Southwest*. See what kind of conclusions they draw based on those facts.

TEXT STRUCTURE Invite students to look at the captions and chapter headings, and ask them how these features help them understand the book. Suggest that students use text structure to help them better understand the book.

ADDITIONAL SKILL INSTRUCTION

GRAPHIC SOURCES Remind students that *graphic sources* are pictures, captions, headings, maps, and more that aid comprehension by putting information into visual form. Direct students' attention to the photograph and caption on pages 8–9 and ask students how this graphic source helps them better understand what goes on at a dude ranch.

Draw Conclusions

- To **draw a conclusion** means to make a decision or form an opinion that makes sense after you think about facts or details.

Directions Below are three conclusions about *Ranches in the Southwest*. Go back to the book and find supporting details for each conclusion.

1. **Conclusion:** The U.S. government needed to force ranchers to graze their cattle in different areas.

Supporting Details: _____

_____

_____

2. **Conclusion:** Guests can have a lot of fun at dude ranches.

Supporting Details: _____

_____

_____

3. **Conclusion:** Ranching life is hard.

Supporting Details: _____

_____

_____

4. After reading *Ranches in the Southwest*, what conclusions can you draw about how you would like living on a ranch?

_____

_____

_____

_____

Name _____

Vocabulary

Directions Underline the sentence in which the word is used correctly. Then write a sentence of your own.

The coyote was bawling for its mother.
The bawling coyote was so quiet we didn't even know it was there.

1. Your sentence: _____

_____

Wild coyotes live high in the mountains.
My sister had a coyote in her lunchbox.

2. Your sentence: _____

_____

We had a delicious dinner of rice and dudes last night.
Sometimes they call guys "dudes."

3. Your sentence: _____

_____

Please roundup all the beds and then wash the dishes.
At the roundup, all the cattle were put into pens.

4. Your sentence: _____

_____

The cowboy never used his spurs on his horses.
The spurs were not enough to pay for the food.

5. Your sentence: _____

_____

What It Takes to Stage a Play

SUMMARY This nonfiction book examines all the technical aspects of staging a play, including costumes, sets, lighting, and special effects. It also discusses the role of the director as auditions are held, cast members are chosen, and rehearsals begin.

LESSON VOCABULARY

advice
arrangements
dishonesty
snag
arguments
descendant
script

INTRODUCE THE BOOK

INTRODUCE THE TITLE AND AUTHOR Discuss the title and the author of *What It Takes to Stage a Play*. Ask students to predict what the book might be about based on the title and the cover photograph.

BUILD BACKGROUND Ask students if they have ever seen or been part of a play. Ask them what they think happens before the play can be presented and what happens behind the scenes during the play. Based on their impressions, ask students what other information they think they might learn from the book.

PREVIEW/USE TEXT FEATURES Suggest that students look through the book and study the photographs and captions. Ask students what information the photographs and captions give them about putting on a play.

READ THE BOOK

SET PURPOSE Have students set a purpose for reading *What It Takes to Stage a Play*. Students' interest in plays should help guide this purpose.

STRATEGY SUPPORT: ANSWER QUESTIONS Remind students that good readers know where to find the answers to questions about what they read. They might find the answer in just one sentence or in several places, or they may need to use prior knowledge combined with information from the text. Write the following questions on the board: What are the roles of the costume crew, technical director, and stage manager? What things is the director responsible for? What is the author trying to tell me? Have students answer these questions as they read the book. Help them use the answers to draw conclusions about the things that have to happen in order to stage a play.

COMPREHENSION QUESTIONS

PAGE 4 Why are the costumes an important part of the play? *(The costumes help the characters in a play look real.)*

PAGE 7 What are some of the things the stage manager is responsible for? *(The stage manager is responsible for lighting, special effects, and knowing when to change the scenery.)*

PAGES 8–13 What conclusion can you draw about the role of the director of a play? *(The director has the most responsibility for the play. He or she chooses the actors, conducts rehearsals, and may have to settle arguments between the people that work on the play.)*

PAGE 14 What does the business manager do? *(The business manager handles all of the expenses for the play and balances the budget.)*

REVISIT THE BOOK

READER RESPONSE

1. Possible response: Conclusion: Staging a play requires a lot of effort from many different people; Details: The costume crew designs and sews the costumes; the actors try out and perform the play; the business manger handles expenses.

2. Possible response: I want to know what types of things the technical director is responsible for. I can find the answers by reading page 5.

3. Responses will vary but should reflect an understanding that the business manager controls the play's money, and a dishonest business manager would hurt the play if he or she were to steal or misuse the money.

4. Responses will vary.

EXTEND UNDERSTANDING Have students look at the photographs and captions on pages 4–5. Ask them to describe the importance of costumes to a play. Explain that reading captions is often a quick and concise way to get information about a subject described in a text.

RESPONSE OPTIONS

WRITING Have students write a short review of a play or a movie they have seen. Have them think about the way the costumes, scenery, and special effects added to the overall performance.

DRAMA CONNECTION

Provide students with copies of age-appropriate plays. Have students work in groups to draw pictures of what the characters would look like in costume, or what the stage would look like for a particular scene. If desired, assign parts to students and have them read a portion of the play aloud.

Skill Work

TEACH/REVIEW VOCABULARY

Assign each vocabulary word to a group of students. Have each group define its word and identify the word's part of speech. Then have each group use the word in a sentence. Have groups share their definitions, parts of speech, and sentences with the class.

ELL Have students work in pairs to find the vocabulary words in the book and deduce their meanings from the context. Have them check their answers against the Glossary.

TARGET SKILL AND STRATEGY

DRAW CONCLUSIONS Remind students that *drawing a conclusion* means reaching a decision after thinking about the facts in what they read. Give students examples of facts and some conclusions that a person can draw from them. As they read, have students draw conclusions about the work involved in staging a play.

ANSWER QUESTIONS Review with students that when they *answer questions* about a text, it helps to know what type of question is being asked. Explain that sometimes an answer to a question may be found right in the text. Other times a reader needs to use prior knowledge to answer a question. Remind students that answering questions about a text can help them draw conclusions.

ADDITIONAL SKILL INSTRUCTION

GENERALIZE Remind students that when they *generalize*, they are making a broad statement that applies to several things or ideas in a text. Review clue words that signal generalizations (*many, most, all, always, never,* and *none*). Have students each choose one of the roles discussed in the book—costume crew, technical director, stage manager, director, or business manager. When students have finished reading, have them make a generalization about their chosen role.

Draw Conclusions

- To **draw a conclusion** means to make a decision or form an opinion that makes sense after you think about facts or details.

Directions Read the following passage adapted from *What It Takes to Stage a Play*. Complete the chart by listing facts from the passage. Then draw a conclusion by making a decision that makes sense about the facts.

The people behind the scenes of a play are called the crew. Some crew members control the show's lighting. The costume crew makes the costumes. The props crew finds the props the actors will use during the play.

The costumes help make the characters in the play look real. Some costumes look like everyday clothes. Other costumes are fancy. Plays about kings and queens need costumes that will transform the actor into a descendant of a royal family.

1. Fact: _____ _____
2. Fact: _____ _____
3. Fact: _____ _____

↓

4. Conclusion: The people behind the scenes of a play _____ _____

Directions Answer the following question about the passage.

5. Why do you think the props crew is important to a play?

_____

_____

Vocabulary

Directions Choose the word from the box that best completes each sentence. Write the word on the line.

Check the Words You Know

___advice   ___arguments   ___arrangements   ___descendant
___dishonesty   ___script   ___snag

1. It is the business manager's job to make sure there is no _____ among the people handling the finances for a play.

2. Sometimes an actor needs _____ on how to make a performance more believable.

3. People working on a play might run into a _____ that they need to fix.

4. Costumes can help an actor look like a _____ of a royal family.

5. It is the director's job to make _____ for holding play auditions.

6. The director may also have to settle _____ that may happen between the actors.

7. The actors must study the _____ carefully and memorize their lines.

Directions The word *dishonest* means "not honest." Think about the meaning of the prefix *dis-* and use it to define the following words.

8. **disagree** _____

9. **disapprove** _____

10. **dislike** _____

Animal Helpers

SUMMARY This book discusses the ways several different animals help humans. It covers traditional service animals, such as horses and dogs, that are trained to help humans, and it also covers animals that are not usually considered helpful to us, such as leeches and snakes.

LESSON VOCABULARY

ambition	infested
landslide	quicksand
resistance	rickety
roamed	vast

INTRODUCE THE BOOK

INTRODUCE THE TITLE AND AUTHOR Discuss with students the title and the author of *Animal Helpers*. Ask students to look at the picture on the front cover. Based on the picture and the title, ask students what information they think this book will provide. Ask: Do you think this will be a book of fiction or nonfiction? Why?

BUILD BACKGROUND Ask students to share what they know about animals that help humans. Encourage them to think about a wide range of ways animals can help us.

ELL Have students talk about how various animals can be trained to help humans.

PREVIEW/USE TEXT FEATURES As students review the book, ask them what the headings tell them about what they are about to read. Discuss what they think they will learn about animal helpers based on the headings. Point out the pictures and captions and ask what additional information these give about animal helpers.

READ THE BOOK

SET PURPOSE Have students set their own purpose for reading *Animal Helpers*. Encourage them to think of questions to which they would like to find the answers as they read. They may, for example, be interested in how animals can help in the home.

STRATEGY SUPPORT: MONITOR AND CLARIFY Encourage students to monitor their comprehension and to use clarifying strategies as they read. Guide them to look for facts about animal helpers as well as any opinions the author may express. Students may ask themselves questions as they read, such as "What is the author trying to tell me?" or "Does this make sense?"

COMPREHENSION QUESTIONS

PAGE 5 What is one new way that horses can help humans? (*Little horses are being trained to guide blind people, as guide dogs are now trained.*)

PAGE 7 Name three things a trained monkey can do to help a disabled person. (*Monkeys can be trained to flip light switches, open containers, and comfort people.*)

PAGES 10–11 How have trained pigeons helped humans? (*In the past, pigeons have been trained to carry messages, especially during wartime. Pigeons have also been trained to find shipwrecks and people lost at sea.*)

PAGE 12 In what ways can parrots help humans? (*Parrots can fetch things and push buttons. One parrot was trained to help a man control his anger.*)

PAGE 13 How do leeches help humans? (*Doctors use leeches to help blood flow and to stop blood from clotting.*)

REVISIT THE BOOK

READER RESPONSE

1. Possible responses: Fact: Scientists put receivers on rats' backs; Opinion: Rats may one day be able to find people in landslides. Fact: Leeches can help blood flow more freely; Opinion: Snakes may be able to help people predict earthquakes.

2. Responses will vary.

3. *Roamed* means "wandered about." The words that helped me understand the word *roamed* include *wild, over, tame,* and *ride.*

4. Responses will vary, but students should provide a reasonable explanation.

EXTEND UNDERSTANDING Have students study the photographs and captions throughout the book. Have them make a list of the various animals and the ways they have helped humans. Have students choose one of the animal helpers and have them do research in the library or on the Internet to learn more about how the animal is trained or used to help.

RESPONSE OPTIONS

WRITING Encourage students to write a brief, detailed report describing what they learned in their research so that they can share their findings with the class.

SOCIAL STUDIES CONNECTION

Time For
SOCIAL
STUDIES

Have students form small groups and research ways that pets such as cats, dogs, and horses have helped humans through history. Have each group present its findings to the class.

Skill Work

TEACH/REVIEW VOCABULARY

Read page 9. Demonstrate to students how you can deduce the meaning of a word from its context. For example, you may point out that you didn't know what *landslide* meant, but by looking at the words around it, you were able to make an educated guess. Check the definition in the Glossary on page 16. Invite student to work in pairs to find the remaining words, deduce the meanings, and check the definitions in the Glossary.

TARGET SKILL AND STRATEGY

FACT AND OPINION Remind students that a *statement of fact* can be proved true or false, and a *statement of opinion* reflects someone's belief. As students read, have them note statements of fact and of opinion from the book. Point out that even in a nonfiction book, they may find statements of opinion. Stress the importance of knowing the difference between fact and opinion.

MONITOR AND CLARIFY As students read, ask them to monitor their comprehension by watching for passages where the text isn't making sense to them. Remind students to use strategies to help them clarify what they are having difficulty with, such as reading on, adjusting reading rate, or rereading and reviewing certain passages.

ADDITIONAL SKILL INSTRUCTION

DRAW CONCLUSIONS Remind students that to *draw a conclusion* means to think about facts and information and then use reason to make a decision. Have students read page 8. Ask: From the information you just read, what conclusions can you draw about rescue dogs? Use details from what you have read to support your answer.

Fact and Opinion

- A **statement of fact** can be proved true or false.
- A **statement of opinion** tells someone's judgment, belief, or way of thinking about something.

Directions Tell whether each of the following sentences is a statement of fact or a statement of opinion.

1. _____ Every pet makes life more pleasant for its owner.

2. _____ Some monkeys can be trained to turn on lights.

3. _____ St. Bernard dogs have saved people in the Alps.

4. _____ Rats are best at finding people or things.

5. _____ Pigeons have been trained to carry messages.

6. _____ Snakes can always tell if an earthquake is about to occur.

Directions Look through *Animal Helpers*. Record one statement of fact and one statement of opinion from the book.

7. **Statement of Fact:** _____

_____

8. **Statement of Opinion:** _____

_____

Vocabulary

Directions Answer each question using a word from the box. Write the word on the line.

> ### Check the Words You Know
>
> ___ambition   ___infested   ___landslide   ___quicksand
> ___resistance   ___rickety   ___roamed   ___vast

1. _____ Which word means the opposite of *sturdy*?

2. _____ Which word refers to a strong desire for fame or power?

3. _____ Which word refers to something that is immense?

4. _____ Which word refers to a mass of earth or rock that slides down a steep slope?

5. _____ Which word refers to something present in large numbers?

6. _____ Which word means the same thing as *wandered*?

7. _____ Which word refers to very deep, soft, wet sand?

8. _____ Which word refers to the act of resisting or opposing?

Directions Use the following words in a sentence.

9. **ambition** _____

_____

10. **rickety** _____

_____

A Trip to Capitol Hill

SUMMARY This book tells the story of a young student's tour of Washington, D.C. The student learns all about the three branches of government: executive, legislative, and judicial. The student visits the Capitol Building, the Library of Congress, the House and Senate Office Buildings, and the Botanic Garden Conservatory.

LESSON VOCABULARY

Constitution	howling
humble	politics
responsibility	solemnly
vain	

INTRODUCE THE BOOK

INTRODUCE THE TITLE AND AUTHOR Discuss with students the title and the author of *A Trip to Capitol Hill*. Based on the title, ask students what kind of information they think this book will provide. Does the photograph on the cover give any further clues?

BUILD BACKGROUND Discuss with students what they know about the nation's capital. If any of the students have visited there, have them describe what they saw. Did they visit the Capitol Building? Which monuments did they see? If they haven't been there before, have students describe what they know about Washington, D.C.

ELL Have students talk about what they know about Washington, D.C.

PREVIEW/USE TEXT FEATURES Encourage students to look at the captions, sidebars, and headings to get a sense of what will be covered in the book.

READ THE BOOK

SET PURPOSE Have students set a purpose for reading *A Trip to Capitol Hill*. Suggest that, as students read, they write down notes about the details of the story and to provide answers for any questions they might have about the U.S. government.

STRATEGY SUPPORT: INFERRING Remind students that when we infer, we use what we already know about a topic combined with information from the text to come up with our own ideas about the text or story. As students read, have them note clues from the text that they think will help them infer what a visitor to Washington, D.C., can learn about the government of our nation.

COMPREHENSION QUESTIONS

PAGE 4 Why did the Founding Fathers give the government a system of checks and balances? *(to prevent any one branch from having too much power)*

PAGE 5 Which branch of the government is responsible for making laws? *(the legislative branch)*

PAGE 5 How many senators does each state have? *(two)*

PAGE 6 How old does person have to be to run for President? *(35)*

PAGE 7 After the President nominates a Supreme Court justice, who approves the nomination? *(the Senate)*

PAGE 11 Which library has more than 29 million books? *(the Library of Congress)*

REVISIT THE BOOK

READER RESPONSE

1. Responses may vary: The Capitol is an important building, worthy of being home to our nation's legislature. Supporting details will vary.
2. Possible response: The Founding Fathers did not want a king or a dictator to rule the country. Keeping that in mind helps me understand the reasons for the branches of government and the buildings that house them.
3. *Politics, policy, police,* and *politician* are related words. The Greek word that *politics* comes from is *polis,* which means "city-state."
4. Responses may vary, but they should include a sound explanation.

EXTEND UNDERSTANDING Encourage students to review the photographs of all the buildings in the book. Which building would each student most want to visit? Encourage them to do further research on that building in the library or on the Internet.

RESPONSE OPTIONS

WRITING Have students write a letter to their senator or representative. Is there some issue or problem in their country, state, or town that they want to speak out about? Have them look up their senator's or representative's address on the Internet. See if the address is in one of the buildings mentioned on page 12 or page 13.

SOCIAL STUDIES CONNECTION

Time For SOCIAL STUDIES

Have students research their senator or representative. How long has that person been in office? What are some of his or her favorite causes? When is the person in Washington, and when is he or she back in his or her home state?

Skill Work

TEACH/REVIEW VOCABULARY

Have students write each vocabulary word and its definition on a note card. Have them draw cards with a partner and use each word they draw in a sentence.

TARGET SKILL AND STRATEGY

MAIN IDEA AND DETAILS Remind students that each text can be boiled down to a number of *main ideas*. Remind students that each of the main ideas may be supported by *supporting details*. As they read this text, have them write down the main ideas and list the supporting details next to each main idea.

INFERRING Remind students that to infer, you combine what you know with text clues to come up with your own ideas. Have students infer one thing about each building described in the book. Have them write their inferences on note cards and share them with classmates.

ADDITIONAL SKILL INSTRUCTION

GENERALIZE Remind students that a *generalization* is a broad statement or rule that applies to many examples. As students read, have them look for clue words such as *many, most, generally,* and *overall* and note whether or not the author is generalizing.

Main Idea and Details

- The **main idea** is the most important idea about the topic of a paragraph, passage, or article.

- **Supporting details** are the small pieces of information that tell more about the main idea.

Directions Reread the following passage from *A Trip to Capitol Hill*. Then answer the questions about the passage below.

> The Founding Fathers tried to make sure that no one person had too much power. They also knew that a growing nation needed a strong government. They wrote the Constitution to deal with these challenges. In it, they outlined three branches, or parts, of government: legislative, executive, and judicial.
>
> Each branch has responsibility for different jobs. Together, the three branches are designed to make sure the government runs smoothly and protects the rights of its citizens. Each branch has the power to challenge the other two branches. This system of checks and balances prevents any one branch from having too much power.

1. What is the main idea of the first paragraph?

_____

_____

2. What is one supporting detail in the first paragraph that tells about this main idea?

_____

3. What is a detail that supports the supporting detail in question 2?

_____

_____

4. What is the main idea of the second paragraph?

_____

_____

5. What is one supporting detail in the second paragraph that tells more about this main idea?

_____

Vocabulary

Directions Fill in the blank with the word from the box that fits the definition.

Check the Words You Know
___Constitution   ___howling   ___humble   ___politics
___responsibility   ___solemnly   ___vain

1. _____ seriously; earnestly

2. _____ document that establishes the basic principles of the U.S. government

3. _____ meek; modest

4. _____ the art or science of governing

5. _____ job; duty; task

6. _____ crying; wailing; shrieking

7. _____ proud; inflated

Directions Write a brief paragraph about a trip to Washington, D.C. Use as many vocabulary words as possible.

_____

_____

_____

_____

_____

_____

Looking for Changes

SUMMARY This nonfiction book informs students about the causes and effects of global warming and how they may be able to help reduce its effects.

LESSON VOCABULARY

apprentice	club	atmosphere
chemical	essay	manufacturing
pressure	scales	

INTRODUCE THE BOOK

INTRODUCE THE TITLE AND AUTHOR Discuss the title and author of *Looking for Changes*. Based on the title and photo on the cover, ask students to describe what kinds of changes they think this book might be about. Ask students why they think the ice in the cover photo looks that way.

BUILD BACKGROUND Ask students if they have been inside a greenhouse or a room set up for a specific climate. Have students share their experiences. Discuss hot and cold temperatures and how they each affect water, land, and the air. Have students think about what happens to an ice cube when it is in the freezer and when it is placed in their warm hands.

PREVIEW/USE TEXT FEATURES Direct students' attention to the photographs and graphic sources of captions, chapters, graphs, and glossary. Discuss with students the importance of these features in helping them understand what they are reading. Have students turn to page 11. Ask students what they think the arrow in the illustration is showing.

READ THE BOOK

SET PURPOSE Have students set a purpose for reading *Looking for Changes*. Ask them to think about the changes they have noticed in their local climate. Ask them to think about ways they can help save Earth.

STRATEGY SUPPORT: IMPORTANT IDEAS Discuss with students that the chapter titles present the important ideas in the book. Have them write each chapter title on a sheet of paper with space under each title for notes. During reading, have students take notes by writing details that support the ideas.

COMPREHENSION QUESTIONS

PAGE 3 What is *global warming*? *(Global warming means that Earth is slowly getting warmer.)*

PAGE 7 What have scientists learned by measuring the thickness of the ice in the Arctic Ocean? *(The Arctic ice is melting a little bit more each year.)*

PAGE 9 How do scientists know Earth is warmer now than 100 years ago? *(They studied temperature records from 100 years ago.)*

PAGES 10–11 What is a greenhouse? How is Earth like a greenhouse? *(A greenhouse lets sunlight in through glass and holds the sun's heat. Earth has too many greenhouse gases that are holding heat and keeping Earth extra warm.)*

PAGES 14–15 How does riding a bike or walking instead of driving a car help save Earth? *(You won't be adding as many greenhouse gases to the air.)*

REVISIT THE BOOK

READER RESPONSE

1. The photos show that the Arctic Ocean is smaller in 2003 than in 1979. Responses may vary but make sure students understand the concept of global warming and its effects.

2. Responses may vary but make sure students' questions are relevant to the changes happening on Earth and/or how they can help reduce the effects. Make sure students' who, what, or where responses connect appropriately to their questions.

3. An apprentice is someone who works under a professional to learn an art or trade. Response sentences may vary but should show understanding of the meaning for *apprentice*.

4. Responses may vary but make sure students include global warming causes and effects as well as ways they can help, such as warmer temperatures, greenhouse gases, glacial ice melting, planting trees, and recycling.

EXTEND UNDERSTANDING Have students look at the illustrations on pages 14–15. Explain to students that writers use images so the readers will make a connection to the text and remember what they read. Ask: If you saw a person riding a bike today, do you think you would remember that they are helping Earth by not adding greenhouse gases to the air?

RESPONSE OPTIONS

ART Have students create posters showing how people can help save Earth. Display the posters in various locations throughout the school to remind others how they can help, too.

SCIENCE CONNECTION

Using ice cubes, a dish with cold water and a dish with hot water, demonstrate for students how much quicker the ice cube melts in the hot water. Explain that, although the ice cube did melt a bit in the cold water, the ice was in a climate closer to what it needs to survive. Discuss how the effect of the warmer water is related to global warming.

Skill Work

TEACH/REVIEW VOCABULARY

Review the vocabulary words with students. Have them write a sentence that includes *Earth* for each vocabulary word.

ELL Have students work in pairs to find the vocabulary words in the book and write the meaning of each word. Have them check their meanings against the glossary.

TARGET SKILL AND STRATEGY

GRAPHIC SOURCES Remind students that *graphic sources* are captions, chapters, charts, glossaries, graphs, illustrations, maps, photographs, and such that help strengthen their understanding of the text. Have students turn to page 11. Review what the arrow shows. Discuss how the whole illustration relates to the text on that page.

IMPORTANT IDEAS Remind students that important ideas are often presented in nonfiction texts through various types of graphic features and through different text structures, such as cause and effect. Have students list the causes and effects of global warming and the greenhouse effect on a T-chart.

ADDITIONAL SKILL INSTRUCTION

FACT AND OPINION Explain that a *statement of fact* is a statement that can be proved true or false. Describe a *statement of opinion* as someone's judgment, belief, or way of thinking. Point out that statements of opinion cannot be proved true or false, but can be supported or explained. Have students read the first sentence on page 12. Discuss why this is a statement of opinion.

Graphic Sources

- **Graphic sources** show information visually and can help you strengthen your understanding of the text. They include captions, chapters, charts, glossaries, graphs, illustrations, and photographs.

Directions Answer the following questions using information from *Looking for Changes*.

1. What do the illustrations and captions on page 7 tell you that is not in the text?

   _____

   _____

2. How does the graph on page 9 prove that Earth is getting warmer?

   _____

   _____

3. What did you learn from the illustration on page 11?

   _____

   _____

4. How does the photo on page 12 help you understand, *Manufacturing goods can put chemicals into the air as well,* from the text?

   _____

   _____

5. Look at the glossary on page 16. What types of information are included to help you understand a word better?

   _____

   _____

Name _____

Vocabulary

Directions Choose the word from the box that best matches each definition. Write the word on the line.

> ## Check the Words You Know
>
> ___apprentice   ___chemical   ___essay   ___pressure
>
> ___atmosphere   ___club   ___manufacturing   ___scales

1. _____ short written work

2. _____ someone who assists a professional

3. _____ to make something

4. _____ a substance made through chemistry

5. _____ a group of people who meet

6. _____ the mixture of gases around a planet

7. _____ the application of force

8. _____ ways to measure

Directions Write a paragraph about global warming and include at least three vocabulary words.

_____

_____

_____

_____

_____

The Gray Whale

SUMMARY Students are introduced to the gray whale and learn about its physical characteristics, habitat, and migration routes.

LESSON VOCABULARY

biologists	bluff
lagoon	massive
rumbling	tropical

INTRODUCE THE BOOK

INTRODUCE THE TITLE AND AUTHOR Discuss with students the title and the author of *The Gray Whale*. Ask students to predict what they will learn about gray whales in this book. Ask: Is this a nonfiction book?

BUILD BACKGROUND Ask students to share what they know about whales. Perhaps they've seen whales in movies or on television, or they may have seen a whale in an aquarium. Begin a KWL chart, recording the information students already know about whales and what they want to know.

PREVIEW/USE TEXT FEATURES Have students look at the Table of Contents on page 3. Ask students what they'll learn in this book. Invite students to look through the book. Point out other text features, such as the photographs, the captions, and the map.

READ THE BOOK

SET PURPOSE Have students set a purpose for reading *The Gray Whale*. Their interest in these marine mammals may drive their purpose. If students are having difficulty setting a purpose, ask them to refer to the KWL chart to remind them of the questions they have about whales.

STRATEGY SUPPORT: TEXT STRUCTURE Remind students that *text structure* refers to the way an author organizes information in a nonfiction book. Guide students to recognize that this book is organized into chapters by topic.

COMPREHENSION QUESTIONS

PAGES 4–5 Find at least one statement of fact and one opinion. *(Possible response: Fact: In 1946, hunting gray whales was stopped. Opinion: People enjoy touching a gray whale.)*

PAGE 5 Why do you think gray whales were hunted almost to extinction? *(Possible response: They travel close to shore, so hunters find them easily.)*

PAGES 6–7 In the picture, what are the patches of white and yellow on the whale? *(whale lice and barnacles)*

PAGES 8–10 Why do you think gray whales need to dive down deep? What helps them dive? *(They need to be able to dive deep to feed on the bottom of the ocean. Their flukes help them.)*

PAGE 10 What is the main idea of this paragraph? Is it clearly stated? What are some supporting details? *(The main idea is how gray whales eat. Yes. They suck up mouthfuls of water and mud from the ocean floor, and baleen filters out tiny shrimp-like animals.)*

PAGE 12 Using the map, describe the migration route of the gray whale. *(They migrate south from near Alaska to the coast of Mexico and back.)*

REVISIT THE BOOK

READER RESPONSE

1. Possible responses: *Opinion:* Massive, gray creature; people enjoy touching a gray whale. *Fact:* Hunting stopped in 1946; gray whales are 36 to 50 feet long.
2. Possible response: They help me quickly identify what I'll be reading about.
3. *Rumbling* means a sound similar to moaning and growling.
4. Possible response: The labels help me know that the fluke is the tail.

EXTEND UNDERSTANDING Have students create an information web to track and categorize the information they learned in *The Gray Whale*. Discuss with students how the book was organized. Does this organization make sense to students? Can they think of other ways to organize the material?

RESPONSE OPTIONS

WRITING Encourage students to add a column to their KWL charts. The column should be titled *More that I want to learn about the gray whale*. Have them write at least three new questions. Ask students where they can look for answers to these questions. Encourage them to research these questions further.

SCIENCE CONNECTION

Have students work in groups to research another type of whale. Encourage them to create a diagram of the whale, labeling its parts, and a map showing where the whale can be found.

Skill Work

TEACH/REVIEW VOCABULARY

Review the vocabulary words with students. Have them write a sentence that includes the word *whale* for each vocabulary word.

ELL Have students work in pairs to find the vocabulary words in the book and deduce their meanings from the context. Have them check their answers against the glossary.

TARGET SKILL AND STRATEGY

FACT AND OPINION Remind students that a *statement of fact* can be proved true or false, and a *statement of opinion* is someone's judgment. Ask students to tell you which of the following statements is a fact and which is an opinion: In 1946 hunting gray whales was stopped. *(Statement of fact)* Gray whales are beautiful creatures. *(Statement of opinion)*

TEXT STRUCUTRE As students read, remind them to pay attention to the *text structure*, or how the book is organized. Point out that the titles for chapters 2–5 are in the form of a question. Ask students how this helped them as they read.

ADDITIONAL SKILL INSTRUCTION

MAIN IDEA AND DETAILS Remind students that the *main idea* is the most important idea about a topic. The main idea may be stated right in the text or it may not be given in a sentence in the text. In this case, students must use their own thinking to find the main idea and put it in their own words. *Supporting details* are the pieces of information that tell more about the main idea. Have students read pages 6–7. Ask students if they can find the main idea. What are some supporting details?

Fact and Opinion

- A **statement of fact** can be proved true or false.
- A **statement of opinion** is someone's judgment.

Directions On the chart below, record the statements of fact and statements of opinion you found in *The Gray Whale*. You may add your own statements of opinion about gray whales.

Statements of Fact	Statements of Opinion
_____	_____
_____	_____
_____	_____
_____	_____
_____	_____

Directions After learning about gray whales, what do you think of them? Do you like them or not? Why? On the lines below, write your opinion of gray whales. You may include phrases such as "in my opinion" or "I think" to make clear what your opinions are. Be sure to back up your statements of opinion with statements of fact.

_____

_____

_____

_____

_____

_____

_____

Vocabulary

Directions Choose the word from the box that best matches each clue. Write the word on the line.

> ### Check the Words You Know
>
> ___biologists   ___bluff
> ___lagoon   ___massive
> ___rumbling   ___tropical

1. _____ This type of steep slope can often be found on the edge of an island.

2. _____ The sun can shine directly overhead in this region.

3. _____ Something like this would be hard to move.

4. _____ These scientists study plants and animals.

5. _____ This small body of water is found near tropical islands.

6. _____ This is a thunderous sound.

Directions Choose the word from the box that belongs in each group.

7. pond, pool, _____

8. sweltering, hot, _____

9. large, bulky, _____

10. thundering, rolling, _____

11. cliff, mountainside, _____

12. scientists, researchers, _____

Directions Write sentences using each word in the box.

13. _____

14. _____

15. _____

16. _____

17. _____

18. _____

Day for Night

SUMMARY This book explains how Earth moves in relation to the sun and how this movement produces night and day.

LESSON VOCABULARY

brilliant	chorus
coward	gleamed
shimmering	

INTRODUCE THE BOOK

INTRODUCE THE TITLE AND AUTHOR Discuss with students the title and the author of *Day for Night*. Encourage students to comment on the photograph on the cover and how it relates to the title. Ask them how day and night might relate to science.

BUILD BACKGROUND As a class, complete a Venn diagram about night and day. Guide students to think of a variety of similarities and differences. For example, ask: What are typical daytime jobs, and what are typical nighttime jobs?

PREVIEW/USE TEXT FEATURES Draw students' attention to the table of contents. Ask: How does the table of contents help us predict what the book will be about? Encourage volunteers to share their predictions and write them on the board. Prompt students to preview the rest of the book and confirm their predictions by reading the captions and looking at the photographs and diagrams.

READ THE BOOK

SET PURPOSE Prompt students to set a purpose for reading by looking at the table of contents. Ask: How do the chapter titles relate to night and day? Which chapter are you most interested in reading? What do you hope to find out as you read?

STRATEGY SUPPORT: VISUALIZE Students can *visualize* to help them understand scientific concepts. After students have read page 11, ask them to visualize Earth spinning on its axis like a top.

COMPREHENSION QUESTIONS

PAGE 6 Would Ptolemy's idea explain day and night? *(Possible response: Yes, because as the sun traveled around Earth, there would still be day and night.)*

PAGE 10 How does the shape of Earth's orbit affect the distance between Earth and the sun? *(Possible response: Since the shape is an oval, Earth's path does not keep a constant distance from the sun.)*

PAGE 13 What words in the paragraph help you visualize night by a campfire? *(Possible response: new sounds, chorus, chirp, fly, dark sky.)*

PAGE 14 Are most humans diurnal or nocturnal creatures? Why? *(Diurnal; most humans sleep during the night and wake during the day.)*

REVISIT THE BOOK

READER RESPONSE

1. Possible response: The bodies of nocturnal creatures are adapted to night living. Diurnal creatures are most active during the day.
2. Possible response: path, oval-shape, angle, tilt.
3. Possible responses: the moon, near planets, or even something unrelated to the book's topic.
4. Possible response: I can see how Earth spins on its axis as it moves around the sun.

EXTEND UNDERSTANDING Explain to students that that the diagram on pages 10–11 is like a multiple exposure photograph taken over the course of a year. Help students understand that there are not, in fact, four Earths; this diagram shows the position of Earth at four different points in time during the year. Lead students to see that there is a time lapse of approximately three months between each position.

RESPONSE OPTIONS

WRITING Ask students to write about whether it would be better to be awake during the day or during the night and why.

ELL Lead a writing activity that uses sentence frames. Write the following sentence frames on the board: "At night there is _____." "In the day you can _____." Have students write as many variations as they can.

SCIENCE CONNECTION

Have students keep a journal about what they observe around them in the day and in the night for a few days. Prompt them to organize their entries by the senses of sight, smell, and sound.

Skill Work

TEACH/REVIEW VOCABULARY

Write each word on a card and fold each card. Put all cards into a hat or box. Have each student draw one card and use the word in a sentence. Once all cards are drawn, repeat the activity; this time have each student draw two words and use them in a sentence.

TARGET SKILL AND STRATEGY

GENERALIZE Remind students that to *generalize* is to make a broad statement or rule that applies to many examples. Ask students to identify a generalization made by the author on page 6. *(Most people agreed with Ptolemy's ideas about Earth being the center of the universe.)* Have students look for clue words *(all, none, most, usually)*.

VISUALIZE Explain that when readers *visualize,* they imagine pictures of what they are reading. Remind students to visualize as they read descriptive text. Visualization can also help students make generalizations. Prompt students to practice this skill on pages 4–5. Say: Read the first paragraph and visualize sitting at a campfire. Now make a generalization about how the sun and a campfire are similar. *(The sun and a campfire are both sources of light and heat.)*

ADDITIONAL SKILL INSTRUCTION

CAUSE AND EFFECT The text on page 15 contains several *cause-and-effect* relationships that may be difficult for students to recognize, because there are few clue words. Draw a cause-and-effect graphic organizer on the board. Complete the chart with students.

Generalize

- To **generalize** is to make a broad statement or rule that applies to many examples.
- Generalizations can contain clue words such as *most, all, always,* and *never.*
- A **valid** generalization is supported by examples and is accurate. A **faulty** generalization is not supported by examples and does not make sense.

Directions Read the following passage. Then answer the questions below.

It took a long time for people to accept Copernicus's ideas. In the 1600s, Johannes Kepler wrote about the planets and their movements. He agreed with Copernicus. Galileo, a scientist from Italy, used a telescope to prove Copernicus was right.

Powerful people became angry. They wanted Galileo to say Copernicus was wrong. Galileo believed he was right and did not want to be a coward. He refused and was banned from publishing his writings.

Copernicus, Kepler, and Galileo were right. By the end of the 1600s, most people believed that Earth moved around the sun.

1. What generalization does the author make?

_____

_____

2. What generalization can you make about Copernicus, Kepler, and Galileo?

_____

_____

What are three facts or examples that support your generalization?

3. _____

4. _____

5. _____

Vocabulary

Directions Synonyms are words that have similar meanings. Draw a line to match the synonyms.

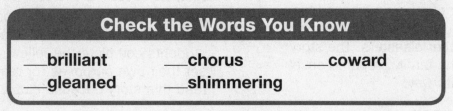

Check the Words You Know

___brilliant   ___chorus   ___coward
___gleamed   ___shimmering

1. brilliant   **a.** twinkling—giving off flickering light

2. chorus   **b.** yellow-belly—someone who is afraid

3. coward   **c.** choir—a group of people who sing together

4. gleamed   **d.** radiant—giving off bright steady light

5. shimmering   **e.** beamed—shone light in one direction

Directions Use each word below in a sentence.

6. brilliant

_____

7. coward

_____

8. gleamed

_____

9. shimmering

_____

10. chorus

_____

Surviving Hurricane Andrew

SUMMARY *Surviving Hurricane Andrew* is a fictional account of a young boy and his family living through one of Florida's most memorable weather disasters. The story describes how the family prepared once Andrew was on its way.

LESSON VOCABULARY

destruction	expected	forecasts
inland	shatter	surge

INTRODUCE THE BOOK

INTRODUCE THE TITLE AND AUTHOR Discuss with students the title and the author of *Surviving Hurricane Andrew.* Point out the genre as fiction. Ask: What are the people in fiction stories called? (*characters*) What else besides characters do you expect to find in a work of fiction? (*Possible responses: a story with a beginning, middle, and end; some kind of problem; pictures*)

BUILD BACKGROUND Draw a concept web on the board with the word *hurricane* in the center. Have students brainstorm all the words that come to mind when they think of the term *hurricane*. Once students have finished the brainstorming activity, have a volunteer look up the definition of the word *hurricane* in a dictionary. As a class, compare the ideas in the concept web to the definition.

ELL If any students have lived through hurricanes in their home countries, have them talk about the experience with their classmates. Invite students to describe the weather, their preparations, their actions during the storm, and the aftermath.

PREVIEW/USE TEXT FEATURES Have students flip through the book, looking at the pictures. Discuss who they think the main characters are and what they think may happen based on the pictures and title.

READ THE BOOK

SET PURPOSE Discuss with students why many people read fictional stories. Then have students complete the following sentence to set their own purposes for reading: I want to read this story because I _____.

STRATEGY SUPPORT: PREDICT AND SET PURPOSE Help students make *predictions* about the text based on the graphics in the book. Ask them: What do you think the characters do in the first part of the book? What do you think happens later in the book? Explain that reading to confirm their predictions is *setting a purpose* for reading.

COMPREHENSION QUESTIONS

PAGE 5 Make a prediction about whether the father is right about the weekend. (*Possible response: No, the weather will not be nice because Hurricane Andrew will come.*)

PAGES 10–11 What do the graphics on these pages show you that is not in the text? (*how a hurricane forms and what Hurricane Andrew looked like*)

PAGES 12–13 At this point in the story, who are some of the important characters? How do you know? (*Possible responses: the boy, because he is telling the story; Gramps, because he knows a lot about hurricanes*)

PAGE 14 Make a prediction about what will happen to the family and their house. (*Possible response: They will be fine because the house is inland, and Gramps and Dad know what to do.*)

PAGE 15 How does the picture on this page help you understand the ending of the story? (*Possible response: It shows how bad the damage was from the tree that fell in the story.*)

REVISIT THE BOOK

READER RESPONSE

1. Responses will vary, but students should change one event from the story and show how it affects the rest of the story.
2. Possible response: If Mom could not get duct tape, the narrator and Gramps would not have been able to tape the windows, and the windows might have shattered.
3. Possible responses: howling, screeching, breaking, cracking, falling, whistling, pounding
4. Responses will vary.

EXTEND UNDERSTANDING Explain to students that the setting in a work of fiction is the time and place in which events happen. Point out that the setting often affects what happens to the characters in a story, just as it does in this story. Have students add a *Setting* section to their *Important Elements* chart that includes *Plot* and *Characters*. (See *Additional Skill Instruction* at right.) Have students describe when and where the story takes place.

RESPONSE OPTIONS

WRITING Tell students to write the story of Hurricane Andrew as if it were one of Gramps's favorite hurricane stories. Suggest to students that they review the events in the selection, particularly page 6, to help them write their stories from Gramps's point of view.

SCIENCE CONNECTION

Tell students to choose one story about someone who lived through the hurricane and write a summary of what happened.

Skill Work

TEACH/REVIEW VOCABULARY

Write the vocabulary words on a set of index cards, and tape the cards to the board in a column in random order. Then write the definitions on the board in a list. Make sure the definitions are not in the same order as the words. Have volunteers try to move each vocabulary word to its correct definition by using word analysis and educated guesses. At the end of the activity, move any misplaced words to their correct spots.

TARGET SKILL AND STRATEGY

CAUSE AND EFFECT Remind students that a *cause* is why something happened; the *effect* is what happened. Discuss clue words such as *because* and *so* that signal why something happened or what happened. (*Because it was raining, the cars got wet. It was raining, so the cars got wet.*)

PREDICT AND SET PURPOSE Remind students that when they *predict,* they are guessing what will happen next in a selection. Explain that looking at graphic sources before they read can help them make predictions about a story. Have students look through the graphics to make predictions about the story and the characters. Encourage them to read for the purpose of confirming their predictions.

ADDITIONAL SKILL INSTRUCTION

PLOT AND CHARACTER Review with students that *plot* is what happens in a story. Remind students that a plot has a beginning, middle, and end. Review that *characters* are the people who take part in the action of a story. Remind students that not all characters are important to the plot. To help students track the plot and important characters in the selection, have them complete an *Important Elements* chart. The chart should include *Plot* and *Characters* sections.

Cause and Effect

- A **cause** is why something happened; an **effect** is what happened.
- Clue words such as *because* and *so* may signal a cause-and-effect relationship

Directions Read the sentences. Underline the effect and circle the cause.

1. The sand spit helps make the waves smaller, so it is safer for people to swim.

2. Scamp was barking at the whistling wind, so I picked him up and held him.

3. The windows didn't shatter because we used duct tape to put Xs on them.

Directions Use *Surviving Hurricane Andrew* to answer the questions on the lines provided.

4. What is the cause of the RV being on its side on page 15?

_____

_____

_____

5. What is the effect of the cooler being filled with ice on page 9?

_____

_____

_____

Vocabulary

Directions Unscramble each of the clue words using the definitions. Take the letters that appear in circles and unscramble them for the answer to the final clue.

> ### Check the Words You Know
> ___destruction   ___expected   ___forecasts
> ___inland   ___shatter   ___surge

1. thought something would happen

   TEPDECXE

2. predictions

   OETSCSFAR

3. in or toward the interior

   DALNIN

4. to break into pieces suddenly

   RESTATH

5. a sweep or rush, especially of waves

   SEGUR

6. What does a hurricane cause?

Directions Write a story about a hurricane. In your story, use each of the vocabulary words in the box.

_____

_____

_____

_____

_____

_____

_____

Saving Trees by Using Science

SUMMARY This book examines the various threats to forests around the world including disease, insects, climate, and the increased need people have for wood. It explores some of the ways people are working to ensure that forests will continue to thrive in the future.

LESSON VOCABULARY

announcement	feature
harness	lumberjacks
requirements	thaw
unnatural	untamed

INTRODUCE THE BOOK

INTRODUCE THE TITLE AND AUTHOR Discuss with students the title and the author of *Saving Trees by Using Science.* Have students share thoughts about why they think trees might need saving.

BUILD BACKGROUND Have students describe the various ways trees are used. They will likely mention things such as for fruit, shade, and to provide lumber for building. Ask students if they can think of reasons that forests might be in danger. Responses will likely include fires, changing weather patterns, and diseases that strike trees.

PREVIEW/USE TEXT FEATURES Encourage students to look at the photographs, captions, and headings to get a sense of what will be covered in the book.

READ THE BOOK

SET PURPOSE Have students set a purpose for reading *Saving Trees by Using Science.* Suggest that as students read, they write down notes to summarize the story and to provide answers for any questions they might have about saving trees.

STRATEGY SUPPORT: INFERRING Remind students that when we *infer*, we use the information in a text and what we already know to come up with our own ideas. Model making an inference on page 5 of *Saving Trees by Using Science.* Say: The text says that human activity is the greatest factor for trees disappearing. I know that people cut down trees for lumber and to clear space for houses. These must be some of the activities that the author is referring to.

COMPREHENSION QUESTIONS

PAGE 4 Which countries have more land covered by forests than the United States? *(Brazil, Russia, and Canada)*

PAGE 6 Why is there a greater demand for lumber today than ever before? *(The world's population is larger, so there are more people who want products made from wood.)*

PAGE 7 Other than an increased need for lumber, what are some other threats to trees? *(Fire, plant diseases, and some insects are the three biggest threats to trees.)*

PAGE 11 What is *silviculture*? *(Silviculture is the science of growing trees and taking care of them.)*

PAGE 15 How can we all help to save our forests? *(We can all help to save our forests by planting new trees and by recycling paper and other products made from lumber.)*

REVISIT THE BOOK

READER RESPONSE

1. Possible response: Generalization: Trees are disappearing from forests. Specific problems: Fires are destroying trees. Diseases and insects are destroying trees. People are cutting down too many trees.
2. Responses will vary.
3. *featuring, harnessing,* and *thawing;* Sentences will vary but should reflect the correct use of each word.
4. Reponses will vary.

EXTEND UNDERSTANDING Have students look at the maps on page 5. Help them see that the maps show how forested areas changed from 1850 to 1992. Ask: How do these maps help you understand the problem our forests have been facing?

RESPONSE OPTIONS

WRITING Invite students to write about ways their lives might be affected if people don't work together to save our forests.

SCIENCE CONNECTION

Encourage students to do additional research to learn more about the efforts being made to save our country's forests. Suggest that they look into other ways that people are working to clean up the environment and protect other natural resources.

Skill Work

TEACH/REVIEW VOCABULARY

As you say each vocabulary word, have students who know what the word means offer definitions to the rest of the class.

ELL Have students make a flashcard for each vocabulary word. Guide them to write the word on one side of the card and the definition on the other. Encourage them to use the book's Glossary to help with the definitions. Then have students work in pairs to quiz each other on the words using the flashcards.

TARGET SKILL AND STRATEGY

GENERALIZE Remind students that an author may present ideas about several things or people and sometimes make a statement about all of them together; this is a *generalization.* Point out that clue words such as *most, all, always,* and *never* identify generalizations. Inform students that *valid generalizations* are supported by facts and logic, whereas *faulty generalizations* are not. Have students look for generalizations as they read and determine whether each is valid or faulty.

INFERRING Remind students that combining what you already know with text clues to come up with your own ideas is called *inferring.* Encourage students to make inferences as they read. After reading, have students share what they were able to infer about the text.

ADDITIONAL SKILL INSTRUCTION

MAIN IDEA AND DETAILS Remind students that the *main idea* is the most important idea about a topic. Explain that sometimes the main idea in a nonfiction work will be given as a single sentence within a passage. Sometimes students will have to figure it out on their own. After students have read *Saving Trees by Using Science,* have them work in small groups to create "Main Idea and Supporting Details" webs. Compare and discuss the webs as a class.

Name _____

Generalize

- When an author presents ideas or facts about several things or people and makes a statement about all of them together, this is a **generalization**.

- Sometimes clue words, such as *most, all, always,* and *never,* help identify generalizations.

- **Valid generalizations,** based on facts, are accurate; **faulty generalizations** are not.

Directions Read the following passage. On the graphic organizer below, write four supporting facts about the importance of rain forests—one in each oval. Then, in the middle oval, write the generalization that the author has reached.

Rain forests will always play an important role in our world. Do you like chocolate? How about chewing gum? Thank the tropical rain forest trees that make the ingredients. Rain forests are a huge source of food. Fruits such as mangoes and bananas come from rain forests. Many medicines also come from the rain forests, including 25 percent of the ingredients in today's cancer drugs.

One-fifth of the world's fresh water is in the Amazon rain forest. And the rain forests affect rainfall, which in turn affects climate around the world. The rain forests have been called the "lungs" of the planet because they provide 20 percent of the world's oxygen. Finally, more than half of the world's species of plants, animals, and insects live in the rain forests.

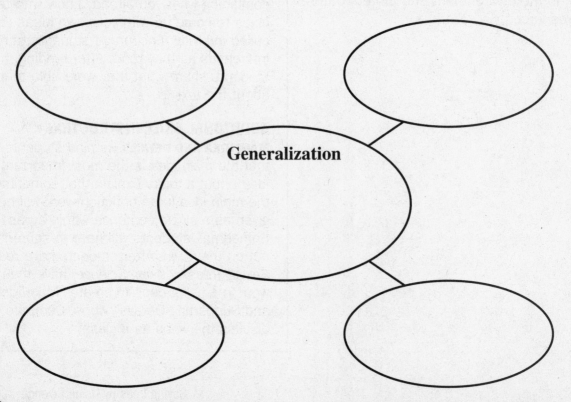

Generalization

Name _____

Vocabulary

Directions Read each definition. Write the word from the box that has the same meaning as the word or phrase.

Check the Words You Know

___announcement	___feature	___harness	___lumberjacks
___requirements	___thaw	___unnatural	___untamed

---

1. _____ things that are needed

2. _____ to control and put to use

3. _____ act of announcing or making known

4. _____ wild; not obedient

5. _____ distinct part or quality

6. _____ people whose work is cutting down trees

7. _____ to melt anything frozen

8. _____ not natural; not normal

Directions Write two sentences below. Use one word from the box above in each sentence.

9. _____

_____

_____

10. _____

_____

_____

Mini Microbes

SUMMARY This book tells about microscopic forms of life called microbes that exist everywhere on Earth, such as in the air, water, soil, and even the human body. The author explains that microbes are much more helpful and much less harmful than people think.

LESSON VOCABULARY

analysis	beakers
hollow	identify
lecture	microscope
precise	relentless

INTRODUCE THE BOOK

INTRODUCE THE TITLE AND AUTHOR Discuss the title and author of *Mini Microbes*. Based on the title and the photograph on the cover, ask students to predict what they think this book might be about. Ask students why they think the author chose this photo for the cover of the book and what they think these microbes look like. *(Possible response: They look like oranges and tree branches.)*

BUILD BACKGROUND Explain that germs are microbes. Have students give examples of the ways people keep from passing germs, such as covering their mouths when they sneeze or cough and surgeons wearing masks to cover their noses and mouths. Discuss ways people remove germs, such as washing their hands and washing fruits and vegetables.

PREVIEW/USE TEXT FEATURES As As students page through the book, point out the Glossary in the back of the book. Direct their attention to the vocabulary words highlighted in yellow throughout the text. Explain that these words are defined in the glossary. Then point out the captions that accompany the photographs. Discuss what students think they will learn about microbes based on the captions.

READ THE BOOK

SET PURPOSE Have students set a purpose for reading *Mini Microbes*. Ask them to think about how our lives are affected each day by things in our bodies that we cannot see.

STRATEGY SUPPORT: VISUALIZE Have students choose a description from the book that they can visualize. Have them write down the description in the center of a web. In the surrounding circles, have students write down the images they have formed in their minds. Have students present their webs to the class and explain how descriptive words helped them visualize images in the selection.

COMPREHENSION QUESTIONS

PAGE 3 Why do you think the author titled his book *Mini Microbes*? *(He called the microbes "mini" microbes because they are tiny.)*

PAGE 7 Why does the moldy bread fall apart? *(The microbes have eaten most of the bread, so there is hardly any of it left.)*

PAGES 8–9 How does dough with yeast differ from dough without yeast? *(The dough with yeast becomes light, fluffy bread because the yeast causes the dough to rise. The dough without yeast remains thin and flat.)*

PAGE 11 Which words help you visualize what happens when microbes give off waste products? *(Possible response: The word slime helps me picture a slippery, rotten banana covered in a sticky, smelly liquid.)*

PAGE 14 Why do scientists want the microbes to reproduce faster? *(They know that it takes lots of microbes to eat up all of the oil from an oil spill.)*

REVIST THE BOOK

READER RESPONSE

1. Possible responses: Helpful: help make food; make soil; produce food for other creatures; produce oxygen; Harmful: spoil food; produce germs that make us sick
2. Possible responses: I see a close-up of round microbes eating drops of oil. In my mind, I see the oil spill getting smaller and smaller until it disappears.
3. Possible responses: Scientists can pour liquids containing microbes into a beaker.
4. Possible responses: Microbes are all around us and inside of our bodies. It is important to learn about all the ways microbes can help us.

EXTEND UNDERSTANDING Point out that the first mass production and administration of penicillin occurred during World War II and that it saved the lives of many American soldiers. Explain that penicillin fought off infectious diseases and made open-heart surgery, burn management, and organ transplants possible for the first time ever. Discuss with students how wartime conditions would have been different without the discovery of penicillin.

RESPONSE OPTIONS

WRITING Encourage students to write a paragraph explaining how microbes are responsible for many of the foods we eat.

SCIENCE CONNECTION

TIME FOR Science

Have students conduct research to find out about the effects of mold, such as rotten wood, stains on furniture and other belongings, damaged buildings, and mold allergies. Have students share their research with the class.

Skill Work

TEACH/REVIEW VOCABULARY

Place students into small groups and have them write the vocabulary words and definitions on separate slips of paper. Have students shuffle and spread out the slips word-side up. Have them take turns choosing a word and its matching definition. Students receive one point for each correct match. Repeat the game several times to reinforce word meaning.

ELL Help Spanish-speaking students access the meaning of vocabulary words by pointing out the following cognates: *microscope/microscopio, precise/preciso, analysis/análisis, identify/identifcar,* and *microbe/microbio.* Have students write each vocabulary word on an index card and define each word on the back by drawing pictures or writing words and phrases.

TARGET SKILL AND STRATEGY

COMPARE AND CONTRAST Remind students that to *compare* is to look at how two or more things are alike. To *contrast* is to look at how two or more things are different. Explain that sometimes clue words, such as *but, however, like,* and *both* are used. Point out the clue words *however* and *like* on pages 8 and 9 of *Mini Microbes.*

VISUALIZE Remind students that they can visualize by creating pictures in their minds as they read. Explain that this picture is often created by descriptive details and sensory words. Remind students that identifying descriptive details and sensory words may help them better understand what they read in a text.

ADDITIONAL SKILL INSTRUCTION

FACT AND OPINION Review with students that a *fact* is a statement about something that can be proved true or false. An *opinion* is a person's judgment, belief, or way of thinking about something. Point out that an opinion cannot be proved true or false, but can be supported or explained. Ask students to read the sentence on page 8, *Moldy bread doesn't sound good to eat.* Then discuss why it is a statement of opinion.

Compare and Contrast

Directions Complete the Venn diagram to show the features of both types of microbes.

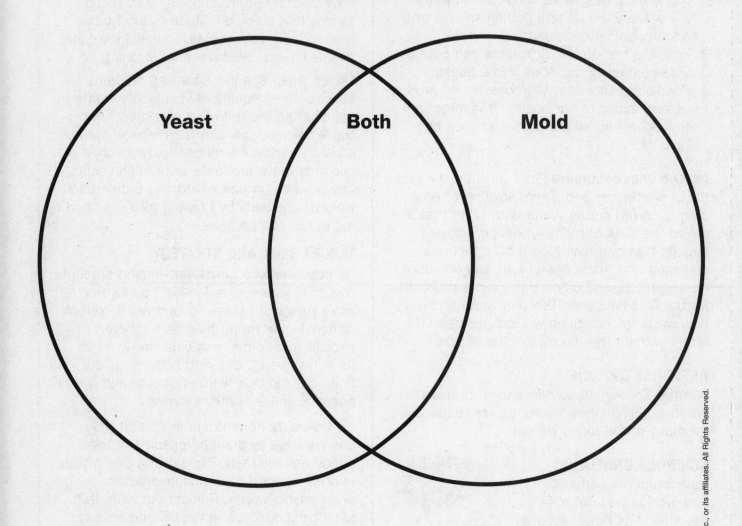

Yeast   Both   Mold

Vocabulary

Directions Read each vocabulary word below. In each blank, write the number of the definition that matches each word. Then complete the word search. Can you find all of the vocabulary words?

VOCABULARY

___ analysis   ___ beakers   ___ hollow   ___ identify

___ lecture   ___ microscope   ___ precise   ___ relentless

DEFINITIONS

1. thin, flat-bottomed glass cups with no handles, used in laboratories
2. having nothing inside
3. very exact or accurate
4. planned speeches or talks, usually for the purpose of instruction
5. a method of studying a thing or determining its essential features
6. tool with lenses for magnifying very small things
7. without pity; harsh
8. recognize

E	L	D	S	R	E	K	A	E	B	R
G	P	M	F	K	Z	V	A	I	Q	E
S	R	O	N	E	R	U	T	C	E	L
I	E	C	C	R	A	Z	Q	O	E	E
S	C	R	S	S	M	X	T	D	J	N
Y	I	T	B	H	O	L	L	O	W	T
L	S	C	R	A	H	R	O	Y	A	L
A	E	K	W	S	L	P	C	J	U	E
N	Y	F	I	T	N	E	D	I	A	S
A	R	X	S	Y	J	M	Q	L	M	S

Dolphins: Mammals of the Sea

SUMMARY This reader introduces various kinds of dolphins, characteristics of the species, growth patterns, and habitats. Students will also read about the humanlike way dolphins whistle and click in their communications.

LESSON VOCABULARY

aquarium	dolphins
enchanted	flexible
glimpses	pulses
surface	

INTRODUCE THE BOOK

INTRODUCE THE TITLE AND AUTHOR Discuss with students the title and the author of *Dolphins: Mammals of the Sea*. Based on the title, ask students to predict if the author has written a fiction or nonfiction book. Talk about why authors will make general titles. Students may suggest that the purpose is to give a basic introduction to the topic. Others may say that they want to distinguish dolphins from other water mammals.

BUILD BACKGROUND Ask students to describe what they know about dolphins and the environment today. Remind students that dolphins are mammals, as are humans. Students may want to extend the discussion by talking about stories they've read or some of the media's presentations of dolphins.

PREVIEW/USE TEXT FEATURES As students leaf through the selection, they will be quickly drawn to the engaging photographs. Draw students' attention to the parts of the dolphin on pages 4–5, and ask them to suggest what the heads in the text tell about what will be in this book.

READ THE BOOK

SET PURPOSE The students themselves should think about why they might like to read about dolphins. Help them to discuss or write this purpose. Ask whether they like animals or swimming and water sports. Or, students may be interested in helping to keep the environment safe for animals, and this selection would give them information on dolphins.

STRATEGY SUPPORT: SUMMARIZE Remind students that *summarizing*, or remembering the important information in a book, can help them keep track of the sequence of events in the selection. As students read, have them pause at the end of each section of the book and summarize the information in that section.

COMPREHENSION QUESTIONS

PAGE 5 Why do dolphins have a blowhole? *(This is how they take in air.)*

PAGE 6 How will a baby dolphin recognize its mother? *(The mother whistles for several days after the baby is born.)*

PAGE 8 In what ways is the bottle-nosed dolphin different from other dolphins? *(Answers will vary but may include that its beak is shaped like a bottle.)*

PAGES 9 AND 10–11 Describe the difference between the bottle-nose dolphin and the hourglass dolphin. *(Bottle-nose dolphins have long beaks and travel in large groups; hourglass dolphins are smaller and travel in small groups.)*

REVISIT THE BOOK

READER RESPONSE

1. Possible response: Dolphins breathe air and are mammals; dolphins are different colors and shapes. Every dolphin is unique.
2. Possible response: The Amazon River dolphin uses pulses of sounds along with the whisker-like hair on its beak to locate food.
3. Possible response: *Pulses* are beats and are edible seeds.
4. Possible response: You can see the dorsal fin on top and pectoral fin on the bottom.

EXTEND UNDERSTANDING Ask students to think about a topic related to dolphins that they would like to learn more about. Take one student's topic and develop the steps of writing about it as a class. Figure out together where to go to research the topic. Be sure to include some fun ways to learn about or experiment with the topic. Then move on to the steps of organizing the information, sometimes using a graphic organizer. Then write one paragraph on the board, which the students dictate to you. Ask for a main idea and supporting details. Ask a volunteer to make up a generalization that sums up the topic.

RESPONSE OPTIONS

WRITING Suggest students make their own graphic organizer of different dolphins.

ELL Lead a writing game to complete a sentence frame such as *I see a* _____. One student points to some element in a photograph in the selection and asks an English language learner to write the word that completes the sentence frame. Have student pairs work on completing several sentence frames.

SCIENCE CONNECTION

TIME FOR Science

Discuss what dolphins can teach us about animal behavior. Ask interested students to prepare a short skit on the ways dolphins move compared with the ways humans move.

Skill Work

TEACH/REVIEW VOCABULARY

Before reading, ask students to guess what each vocabulary word might have to do with dolphins. Ask volunteers to take a vocabulary word and find out how the word is used in the selection. After reading, ask the volunteers to point out what that word added to better understanding some part of the dolphin or its behavior.

TARGET SKILL AND STRATEGY

COMPARE AND CONTRAST Remind students that to *compare* and *contrast* is to look for likenesses and differences. One way writers often organize writing about a science topic is to use a compare-and-contrast approach. When several different kinds of dolphins are presented, readers are able to see both the similarities, or comparisons, as well as the differences, or contrasts. You may want to use a Venn diagram to compare and contrast just two kinds of dolphins, or use a cluster diagram to keep track of several kinds of dolphins.

SUMMARIZE Have students write down a summary sentence for each section, using the section heading as a guide. Model summarizing the first heading by saying, "Some facts about how dolphins communicate are that dolphins have their own special whistle, and that these signature whistles may help dolphins identify who is around them."

ADDITIONAL SKILL INSTRUCTION

GENERALIZE Remind students that a generalization is a broad statement that applies to many examples. In other words, from the many facts and ideas the author has presented on dolphins, students should be able to formulate a generalization about the look and behavior of dolphins. In addition, they should learn to support a generalization with examples from the text.

Compare and Contrast

- To **compare** is to tell how two or more things are alike and also how they are different.
- To **contrast** is to tell only how two or more things are different.

Directions Read the passage below. Then answer the questions.

All dolphins are mammals. Similar to other mammals, dolphins are warm-blooded. They live underwater but have lungs and breathe air. Dolphins all are born live and drink milk from their mothers.

There are many different kinds of dolphins. The bottle-nosed dolphin is found in coastal waters all over the world. Its name comes from the shape of its beak, which is usually a bit more than seven centimeters long. This type of dolphin varies from about two meters to nearly four meters long. These dolphins often travel in groups of 500 to 1000 members. Bottle-nosed dolphins usually have light gray upper bodies with pinkish gray bellies. By contrast, the hourglass dolphin's sharp black-and-white coloring makes it easy to recognize. It is only found in the cold waters surrounding Antarctica. At less than two meters long, it is somewhat smaller than other dolphins. Its black beak is so short that it might not be noticed. Hourglass dolphins travel in tiny groups of 2 to 40 dolphins.

1. Find two similarities among all dolphins.

_____

2. Contrast the coloring of bottle-nosed and hourglass dolphins.

_____

_____

3. Contrast the beaks of bottle-nosed and hourglass dolphins.

_____

_____

4. Compare or contrast where these two types of dolphin live.

_____

_____

Vocabulary

Directions Choose the word from the box that best matches each definition.
Write the word on the line.

Check the Words You Know
___aquarium ___dolphins ___enchanted ___flexible ___glimpses ___pulses ___surface

1. delightful, charming _____

2. short, quick viewings or looks _____

3. building used for showing collections of live fish, water animals and water plants
   _____

4. the top layer _____

5. regular, measured beats _____

6. sea mammals related to the whale, but smaller _____

7. easily bent, not stiff _____

Directions Choose the word from the box that best completes each sentence.
Write the word on the line.

8. The _____ looked like they were skipping as they leapt from
   the water.

9. Some dolphins like to swim very near the _____ of the ocean.

10. The dolphin, with its sleek body and "smiling" face, is an
    _____ animal.

Speaking in Code

SUMMARY This book explores the use of various types of secret codes throughout history with a focus on inventor Samuel Morse and his telegraph. Students will learn that prior to the invention of the telephone, using the telegraph to send Morse code was the fastest way to send messages from one location to another.

LESSON VOCABULARY

advance	developed
exhausting	headquarters
impossible	intense
messages	reveal

INTRODUCE THE BOOK

INTRODUCE THE TITLE AND AUTHOR Discuss with students the title and the author of *Speaking in Code*. Based on the title and cover illustration, ask students to predict if the author has written a fiction or nonfiction book. Some students may recognize the portrait on the cover as Samuel Morse, or they may be familiar with the fact that Morse code uses a series of dashes and dots.

BUILD BACKGROUND Have students discuss what they know about using secret codes or any codes they may know about. Students may have seen numbers assigned to each letter of the alphabet or be familiar with "invisible ink," in which a message must be held up to a hot light or other heat source in order to be read. The shorthand that is often used in sending text messages today can be considered a kind of code.

PREVIEW Ask students to skim through the book looking at the illustrations, labels, and headings. Have students focus on pages 6 and 7 as a clue to what they might learn by reading the book.

READ THE BOOK

SET PURPOSE To help students set a purpose for reading the selections, have them complete the following sentence on their own: I want to read *Speaking in Code* because _____. Suggest to students that they consider the title, the illustrations, the genre, or the author's purpose when deciding why they will read the book.

STRATEGY SUPPORT: IMPORTANT IDEAS Remind students that good readers recognize which ideas they read are the most important. Explain that as students read they should try to identify the most important ideas. Important ideas tell more about the main idea of the book. Model questions to ask while reading, such as: Is this idea important? Or is it a small detail?

COMPREHENSION QUESTIONS

PAGE 7 How does semaphore code work? *(Possible response: Semaphore code uses two flags. Each flag is divided into two colored triangles. The flags are held a certain way to signal each letter of the alphabet. The sender moves the flags to spell out words.)*

PAGE 10 What did Samuel Morse do before he became a scientist? *(Samuel Morse was a painter before he became a scientist.)*

PAGES 14 How did the telegraph change the way people sent messages? *(The telegraph helped messages travel quickly across the country. Railroads became safer with the telegraph system in place. Newspapers could receive news from far away.)*

PAGE 15 Who had an idea for a better telegraph machine? What was that idea? *(Alexander Graham Bell had a better idea for a telegraph machine. That idea became the telephone.)*

REVISIT THE BOOK

READER RESPONSE

1. Possible response: Time line might show significant dates such as invention of semaphore, invention of telegraph, development of Morse Code, invention of telephone in sequence.
2. Possible response: People have used coded messages throughout history. It helped me understand why there are many uses for codes.
3. immature—not mature; imperfect—not perfect; impatient—not patient
4. Responses will vary.

EXTEND UNDERSTANDING Point out that headings in nonfiction organize the facts in a text into groups. Headings also may help the reader understand the main ideas presented in a selection. Discuss with students how the headings in *Speaking in Code* help them understand the main ideas and supporting details of the book.

RESPONSE OPTIONS

WRITING Have students create a code by assigning one number from 1–26 to each letter of the alphabet. Have them use this code to write messages to a partner. Ask the partner to decode the message.

SOCIAL STUDIES CONNECTION

Have students research how some important inventions were discovered, such as the light bulb, the telephone, or the steam engine, and write brief reports describing the inventor's discovery process and how the invention impacted people's lives.

Skill Work

TEACH/REVIEW VOCABULARY

Have students look up the vocabulary words in a dictionary and write down the definitions and parts of speech. Then tell students to write a brief story about secret codes using all the vocabulary words.

ELL Have students work in a group to write a story together. Have one person start the story by writing the first sentence. Then have students pass the story around the group, with each person writing a new sentence. Remind students that the goal is to use as many vocabulary words as they can.

TARGET SKILL AND STRATEGY

SEQUENCE Remind students that keeping track of the *sequence*, or order of events in a book may help them understand the facts that are presented. Write a list of clue words on the board, such as *first, then, meanwhile,* and *now*. Tell students to look for these clue words as they read.

IMPORTANT IDEAS In discussion, have students identify several of the sentences in the book as important ideas or not-so-important ideas. Work with them to make sure they understand the distinction.

ADDITIONAL SKILL INSTRUCTION

AUTHOR'S PURPOSE Remind students that the author's purpose is the reason or reasons an author has for writing a work. Review with students the most common purposes that authors have: to inform, entertain, persuade, or express a feeling or mood. Ask students to make predictions about the author's main purpose for writing *Speaking in Code,* based on the genre of the story *(to inform)*.

Sequence

• **Sequence** is the order of events.

Directions Put this information from *Speaking in Code* in order so that the statements are in the correct sequence. Write the numbers on the lines.

_____ Samuel Morse invented the telegraph.

_____ Alexander Graham Bell invented the telephone.

_____ Don Francisco Salva y Campillo developed a plan to link electrical wires to people in order to send signals.

_____ Semaphore code was developed in France.

_____ In Ancient Greece, messages were sent by writing on the shaved heads of slaves.

_____ Telegrams were used to send important information.

Directions Write about the things you do during a typical day at school. Use the words *first, next, then,* and *finally* to help you.

_____

_____

_____

_____

_____

_____

_____

_____

_____

_____

_____

Name _____

Vocabulary

Directions Draw a line from the vocabulary word to its correct definition.

___advance ___developed ___exhausting ___headquarters
___impossible ___intense ___messages ___reveal

1. advance   **a.** words delivered from one person to another

2. developed   **b.** the main office or center of operations

3. exhausting   **c.** to make something known

4. headquarters   **d.** to move forward

5. impossible   **e.** very strong

6. intense   **f.** brought into being; made

7. messages   **g.** tiring

8. reveal   **h.** not able to be or happen

Directions Unscramble the vocabulary words and then use each one in a sentence.

9. sentein _____

Sentence: _____

10. gemsases _____

Sentence: _____

11. vadcena _____

Sentence: _____

12. bipmsileso _____

Sentence: _____

The Rosetta Stone: The Key to Ancient Writings

SUMMARY This book tells the story of the Rosetta Stone, discovered by Napoleon Bonaparte's troops in 1799. The discovery caused great excitement because scholars knew it could lead to unlocking the secret of Egyptian hieroglyphs. The book also gives a brief overview of ancient Egyptian culture.

LESSON VOCABULARY

ancient	link
scholars	seeker
temple	translate
triumph	uncover

INTRODUCE THE BOOK

INTRODUCE THE TITLE AND AUTHOR Discuss with students the title and author of *The Rosetta Stone: The Key to Ancient Writings*. Ask students to describe the photograph on the front cover. Based on the title and the photo, ask them what they think they will learn about in this book.

BUILD BACKGROUND Ask students to share what they know about Ancient Egypt and Egyptian artifacts. Perhaps they've seen a television show or visited a museum with an Egyptian display. Show the children a page of text written in a language that most of the students in your class don't understand. Ask them how someone could figure out what it says. Ask: What if we found out no one in the world speaks this language anymore?

PREVIEW/USE TEXT FEATURES Invite students to look through the book. Point out the map on page 3. Ask them how the photograph on that page relates to the map. Have students read the headings and look at the photos and pictures in the rest of the book.

READ THE BOOK

SET PURPOSE Have students set a purpose for reading. Their interest in ancient Egypt and Egyptian artifacts may guide their purpose. Or, perhaps they're interested in languages or in solving puzzles. You may suggest that unlocking the secret of hieroglyphics was like solving a very complicated puzzle.

STRATEGY SUPPORT: PREDICT AND SET PURPOSE In discussion, recall with students why it is important to predict what they think a book might be about and to set a purpose for reading. Remind them that previewing can help on both counts.

COMPREHENSION QUESTIONS

PAGE 3 Look at the map. What features do you see? What country is shown? What town? *(Mediterranean Sea, Nile River; Egypt; Rosetta.)*

PAGE 7 What questions did you have about Egyptian hieroglyphics? Where did you find the answers? *(Possible response: What are hieroglyphs? How did they translate them? Answers found on pages 10, 13–15.)*

PAGE 9 What conclusions can you draw about why hieroglyphics died out? *(Possible response: Egypt was ruled by Greeks, only priests used hieroglyphics, so their use was not widespread.)*

PAGE 13 Why would scholars compare the writing on the Rosetta Stone to hieroglyphics on temple walls and sculptures? *(Possible response: They might discover similarities between the two that would help them understand the Rosetta Stone text.)*

PAGE 14 What helped Jean-Francois Champollion figure out hieroglyphics? *(Possible response: He liked learning, was good at languages, interested in Egyptian culture, spent a lot of time studying in Egypt.)*

REVISIT THE BOOK

READER RESPONSE

1. Responses should reflect the glyphs on the chart from page 10.
2. Responses will vary.
3. The prefix *un-* means "not" or "the opposite of." Possible response: unfair, unsure, untie
4. Demotic script is the form of writing in the middle band of the Rosetta Stone.

EXTEND UNDERSTANDING Have students look at the hieroglyphics on the Egyptian stamp on page 10. Ask them to describe some of the images they see. Many of the hieroglyphics are based on symbols that look like animals and people.

RESPONSE OPTIONS

WRITING Encourage students to create their own secret messages in code. They may use our alphabet or symbols. Have them exchange their messages with other members of the class to decode.

SOCIAL STUDIES CONNECTION

Time For SOCIAL STUDIES

Have students research more about the culture of Ancient Egypt. They may choose to explore more about hieroglyphics or day-to-day life or Egyptian art. Have them present their findings to the rest of the class.

Skill Work

TEACH/REVIEW VOCABULARY

Have students look up the vocabulary words in the dictionary. On note cards, have them write the word on one side and the Greek and/or Latin root and the word's definition on the other side. Student pairs may use the cards as flash cards and see how fast they can learn the words.

ELL Point out the word "Mediterranean" on page 3. Tell students that the phrases in the parenthesis tell them how to pronounce the word. Invite students to find other words and their pronunciations in the text. Have students work in pairs to create pronunciations for the vocabulary words.

TARGET SKILL AND STRATEGY

GRAPHIC FEATURES Remind students that *graphic features* are charts, maps, photographs, drawings, and so on, that help strengthen their understanding of the text. Have students read the text on page 3 and then look at the map. Ask what the map shows them. What does the photo show them? Ask: How does the map help you understand what you read in the text?

PREDICT AND SET PURPOSE Invite students to tell you how predicting what they are about to read and setting a purpose for reading can help them be better readers.

ADDITIONAL SKILL INSTRUCTION

DRAW CONCLUSIONS Remind students that when they draw conclusions while reading, they figure something out by thinking about facts and details from what they've read. Have students read page 8. Ask them what conclusions they can draw about Egyptian civilization based on what they just read. (Good farmers, lived well, had lots of goods to trade)

Graphic Features

- **Graphic features** show information visually. They include visual aids such as maps, photographs and captions, time lines, and diagrams. You can use them to help you understand information in the text.

Directions Review *The Rosetta Stone* and write what happened in each year listed below.

1. 196 B.C. _____

2. 30 B.C. _____

3. 1799 _____

4. 1802 _____

5–8. On a separate sheet of paper, make a time line showing these important events.

Name _____

Vocabulary

Directions Use the definitions to solve the puzzle.

Check the Words You Know

___ancient   ___link   ___scholars   ___seeker
___temple   ___translate   ___triumph   ___uncover

Across

2. Victory; success

3. To make known; reveal

4. A building used for worship

5. People who have much knowledge

7. Anything that joins or connects

Down

1. Of times long past

2. To change from one language into another

6. One who tries to find

Top Hat Tompkins, The Detective

SUMMARY In this mystery, Top Hat the Detective needs to help his friend Sid find out what happened to Sid's pet salamanders. Top Hat uses his inquiry and problem-solving skills, along with a little science knowledge, to find the answer to the puzzle.

LESSON VOCABULARY

amphibians	crime
exhibit	lizards
reference	reptiles
salamanders	stumped

INTRODUCE THE BOOK

INTRODUCE THE TITLE AND AUTHOR Discuss the title and the author of Top Hat the Detective. Based on the genre, title, and cover illustration, ask students what type of fictional story they think this will be *(mystery)*.

BUILD BACKGROUND Invite volunteers to tell about times when they lost something important to them. Have students discuss how asking questions and looking at details, or clues, helped them find the missing object.

PREVIEW Have students turn to page 5 in the book and skim the text and look at the picture. Ask what the subject of this mystery seems to be *(salamanders)*. Then have students flip through the remaining pages of the book, stopping at page 15. Tell them not to turn past this page or they might find out the ending of the mystery. Ask: What method does Top Hat, the Detective, seem to use in searching for details about this mystery? *(talking to other kids)*.

READ THE BOOK

SET PURPOSE Review with students their concept web on mysteries. Ask students why people might read mysteries *(to be entertained, to be scared)* and have them set their own purposes for reading this mystery.

STRATEGY SUPPORT: MONITOR AND CLARIFY Have students stop reading periodically in the book. Ask if there was anything they did not clearly understand. Then tell students to read on to see if they can find the answer.

COMPREHENSION QUESTIONS

PAGES 6–7 What information or event on these pages is important to the plot? What is not? *(Possible responses: after the salamanders disappeared, all that was left was a puddle; the butterfly Sid chased was beautiful.)*

PAGE 10 Do you think it is important to the plot that Penny does not sing the correct words to "Twinkle, Twinkle Little Star"? Why or why not? *(Possible response: No, it's not important to the plot because the mystery is about Sid's salamanders, not the words to the song.)*

PAGE 12 In the third paragraph on this page, Top Hat talks about the characteristics of salamanders. Which statements in this paragraph are facts, and which are opinions? Why? *(All of the statements are facts except the last one, because it is Top Hat's opinion that everyone knows salamanders do not have scales. That statement cannot be proved true or false.)*

PAGES 16–17 Based on your prior knowledge of mysteries, did you expect that Top Hat would solve the puzzle? Why? *(Possible response: Yes, because in most mysteries, the detective solves the crime or puzzle.)*

REVISIT THE BOOK

READER RESPONSE

1. Possible responses: Second: Sid ran after a butterfly. Third: Sid found a large puddle when he came back.
2. Possible response: Why is Top Hat Tompkins so successful all the time? I read on in the story to find the answer.
3. Possible response: confused; not able to understand
4. Possible response: I would feel proud that I figured it out and happy that I could help my friend.

EXTEND UNDERSTANDING Explain to students that in mysteries, authors often include events and characters that are not important to the plot just to confuse the reader. Discuss with students why mystery authors would want to confuse readers and how unimportant plot elements may add to the reader's enjoyment of a mystery story. Have students use examples of plot twists in *Top Hat Tompkins, The Detective* to support their answers.

RESPONSE OPTIONS

SPEAKING Divide students into groups, and have each group pick out a scene from *Top Hat Tompkins, The Detective* that they think is important to the plot of the story. Have each group act out its scene for the class and then explain why they thought the scene was important.

SCIENCE CONNECTION

Have students use encyclopedias, the Internet, or other books and resources to learn more about other amphibians like salamanders. Tell students to prepare brief reports about their amphibians in which they include facts about their creatures and their own opinions about the animals.

Skill Work

TEACH/REVIEW VOCABULARY

Put the vocabulary words, their definitions, and parts of speech on the board. Then have students write each word on an index card, with clues about each word on the back of its card. Tell students that they may use dictionaries but not the definitions on the board. Pair students and have each partner give clues until the other guesses the correct word.

ELL Suggest that ELL students play the vocabulary game and act out their clues to help their partners guess the words.

TARGET SKILL AND STRATEGY

CHARACTER AND PLOT Remind students that a *character* is a person or animal in a story. The *plot* is an organized pattern of events in a story that usually includes a beginning, middle, and end. Point out that not all events in a story are important to the plot. As students read, tell them to keep track of characters and any events in the story that are important to the plot.

MONITOR AND CLARIFY Explain that students should periodically *monitor*, or check, their understanding of the text as they read. Explain: When you don't understand something, you can reread that portion or read on in the story to see if it answers your question. Have students monitor their comprehension as they read.

ADDITIONAL SKILL INSTRUCTION

FACT AND OPINION Review with students that a *fact* is a statement about something that can be proved true or false. An *opinion* is a person's judgment, belief, or way of thinking about something. Point out that readers do not actually have to check a statement of fact to decide whether it can be proved true; rather they merely need to know where to look to prove something.

Character and Plot

- A **character** is a person or animal in a story.
- A story's **plot** is the important parts of a story.
- The parts include the **conflict**, the **rising action**, the **climax**, and the **resolution**.

Directions Use the events in the story *Top Hat Tompkins, The Detective*, to list the characters and complete the plot map. Write page numbers to show where you found each event.

Characters: _____

_____

Conflict

↓

Rising Action	
Page _____	Event 1 _____
Page _____	Event 2 _____
Page _____	Event 3 _____
Page _____	Event 4 _____

↓

Climax
Page _____ _____

↓

Resolution
Page _____ _____

Name _____

Vocabulary

Directions Draw a line connecting each word in the left column with its definition in the right column.

1. **stumped**   display

2. **salamander**   confused

3. **lizard**   book of facts

4. **crime**   amphibian

5. **exhibit**   reptile

6. **reference**   unlawful act

Directions Read the words in each group below. Think about each word's meaning and part of speech. Circle the word in each group that does *not* belong in that group.

7. amphibians, salamanders, reptiles

8. lizards, reptiles, salamanders

9. baffled, amphibians, stumped

10. stumped, exhibit, reference

Putting a Stop to Wildfires

SUMMARY This book tells about the wildfire in southern Colorado in July 2005 that threatened to destroy Mesa Verde National Park and examines two types of specially trained firefighters that were called in to battle the fire—*hotshots* and *smokejumpers*.

LESSON VOCABULARY

concentrating	dedication
essential	method
parachute	steer
underbrush	wind

INTRODUCE THE BOOK

INTRODUCE THE TITLE AND AUTHOR Discuss with students the title and author of *Putting a Stop to Wildfires.* Have students look at the cover photograph to anticipate what the book is about.

BUILD BACKGROUND Have students discuss any news reports they may have seen about fires in large outdoor areas such as a national park. Ask them to think about the firefighters that are called in to fight these intense fires. Ask them to share what they know about the gear the firefighters wear and the special training they receive.

PREVIEW/USE TEXT FEATURES As students flip through the book, they will most likely be drawn to the dramatic photographs. Ask students to predict what they might learn about hotshots and smokejumpers based on the photographs, labels, captions, and headings.

READ THE BOOK

SET PURPOSE Have students set their own purpose for reading *Putting a Stop to Wildfires.* Encourage them to think of questions to which they would like to find answers as they read. They may, for example, be interested in the type of training firefighters need to fight wildfires.

STRATEGY SUPPORT: IMPORTANT IDEAS Discuss with students that the chapter headings present the important ideas in the book. Have them write each chapter heading on a note card. During reading, have students take notes by writing details that support the ideas.

COMPREHENSION QUESTIONS

PAGE 3 Why were people in southern Colorado worried about the approaching storm in July 2005? *(The summer had been very dry and hot. Grasses and trees were dry and people worried that lightning would start a fire.)*

PAGE 7 What is a wildfire? *(A wildfire is a fire that burns across a large area of wilderness.)*

PAGE 10 Describe the jackets that hotshots wear. *(Hotshots wear jackets made of materials that don't burn easily. They are usually bright yellow and have broad stripes that catch and reflect light.)*

PAGE 13 How does a smokejumper arrive at a wildfire? *(A smokejumper flies into a burning area in a cargo plane and jumps out wearing a parachute.)*

REVISIT THE BOOK

READER RESPONSE

1. Possible response: to inform readers about how firefighters battle wildfires
2. Possible response: Main idea: Firefighters work hard to battle wildfires. Details: Hotshots and smokejumpers travel all over the country to fight wildfires.
3. Possible response: pens and pencils, textbooks, backpacks
4. Responses will vary.

EXTEND UNDERSTANDING Have students compare the clothing and gear used by hotshots described and pictured on pages 10–11 with the clothing and gear used by smokejumpers described and pictured on page 16. Have them focus on the differences in the clothing and gear and explain the reasons for the differences.

SOCIAL STUDIES CONNECTION

Time For
SOCIAL STUDIES

Have students do research in the library or on the Internet to learn about the firefighters that serve at fire stations in their local community. Ask them to compare and contrast the training local firefighters receive and the gear they wear with those of hotshots and smokejumpers.

Skill Work

TEACH/REVIEW VOCABULARY

Write the vocabulary words on the board. Divide the class into four groups and assign two words to each group. Have each group find its words in the selection and define them using context clues. Ask each group to share its definitions with the class.

ELL Have students make a flashcard for each vocabulary word. Guide them to write the word on one side of the card and the definition on the other. Then have them work in pairs to quiz each other on the words using the flashcards.

TARGET SKILL AND STRATEGY

AUTHOR'S PURPOSE Remind students of the four most common reasons authors have for writing: to persuade, to inform, to entertain, and to express their thoughts and feelings about a topic. Explain that writers may have more than one purpose for writing. Ask students what main purpose or purposes they think the author had in writing *Putting a Stop to Wildfires*.

IMPORTANT IDEAS Remind students that *important ideas* are the facts and details that support the main idea of the story. Encourage students to keep track of important ideas as they read.

ADDITIONAL SKILL INSTRUCTION

FACT AND OPINION Explain that a *statement of fact* is a statement that can be proved true or false. Describe a *statement of opinion* as someone's judgment, belief, or way of thinking. Point out that statements of opinion cannot be proved true or false, but can be supported or explained. Ask students to read the sentence on page 12, *Fighting wildfires is backbreaking work, so these men and women stay in very good shape*. Then discuss why it is a statement of opinion.

Author's Purpose

- An **author's purpose** is the reason or reasons an author has for writing. An author can write to inform, persuade, entertain, or express a mood.

Directions Use *Putting a Stop to Wildfires* to answer the questions below.

1. What do you think is the author's main purpose in writing *Putting a Stop to Wildfires*?

_____

_____

_____

2. Why do you think the author includes the section "Smokejumpers"?

_____

_____

_____

3. Why do you think the author included the labels with the photographs on page 11?

_____

_____

_____

4. How could the story be changed to show a different purpose for writing?

_____

_____

_____

_____

Vocabulary

Directions Choose the word from the box that best completes each sentence. Write the word on the line.

> ### Check the Words You Know
>
> ___concentrating ___dedication
> ___essential ___methods
> ___parachute ___steer
> ___underbrush ___wind

1. It is _____ that hotshots and smokejumpers stay in excellent shape.

2. It takes many hours of _____ to learn to fight wildfires.

3. Smokejumpers jump from cargo planes wearing a _____.

4. You can't fight fires without _____ on where the fire may spread.

5. Sometimes a strong _____ can cause a fire to spread.

6. The men and women who fight wildfires use many different _____ to control the fire.

7. One of the first things hotshots do is clear out trees and _____ that may burn quickly.

8. Smokejumpers learn to jump safely and to _____ themselves while they fall through the air.

Directions Write a short paragraph telling what you have learned about fighting wildfires. Use as many vocabulary words as you can.

_____

_____

_____

_____

_____

Let's Get to Know the Incas

SUMMARY The Incas built an empire and a civilization high in the Andes Mountains around A.D. 1200. They worshipped the sun, built a large capital city and complex irrigation systems, and created a calendar.

LESSON VOCABULARY

curiosity	glorious
granite	ruins
terraced	thickets
torrent	

INTRODUCE THE BOOK

INTRODUCE THE TITLE AND AUTHOR Discuss with students the title and the author of *Let's Get to Know the Incas*. Based on the title, ask students what kind of information they think this book will provide. Ask students to look at the cover and title and explain how the book might be related to the social studies content area.

BUILD BACKGROUND Ask: What ancient cultures can you name? Where were they located? Ask students if they have heard of the Inca culture and know where it was located.

PREVIEW/USE TEXT FEATURES As students preview the book, the illustrations of the ancient Incas and the photos of the current-day people and sites will probably attract their interest. Ask: What can we learn from these text features?

READ THE BOOK

SET PURPOSE Have students set a purpose for reading *Let's Get to Know the Incas*. Students' interest in ancient cultures should guide this purpose. Suggest they read to find out how the lives of people in different levels of Inca society were the same and different. They may also read to find out how lives of ancient Inca people are alike or different from the Inca people of today.

STRATEGY SUPPORT: VISUALIZE Invite students, as they read, to jot down descriptive details that help them visualize with their senses. Challenge them to say which sense each detail appeals to. Invite them to talk about which descriptive details help them picture and remember whatever is being described.

ELL Invite students to draw pictures of people, things, places, or events from the selection that are described with vivid descriptive details. Have children label their drawings and write captions for them. They may wish to include bilingual labels or captions.

COMPREHENSION QUESTIONS

PAGE 5 Where was the Inca government located? *(in the central part of the capital city)*

PAGE 10 How was Inca society organized? *(There were strict levels of power: the Sapa—royal family and advisors; the temple priests, architects, and army commanders; artisans, army captains, farmers, and herders.)*

PAGE 11 What words or phrases in the second paragraph help you visualize details of Inca life? *(Possible responses: men dug holes in the ground; women dropped in seeds; as the maize shoots grew, boys used their slings to frighten birds and animals away from the growing crops.)*

PAGE 12 How did the Inca pay tribute to the emperor? *(by giving food, goods, or labor)*

PAGE 14 What did Spanish explorer Francisco Pizarro hope to find in South America? *(gold and other riches)*

PAGE 16 How is the life of modern Inca people similar to the life of the ancient Inca? *(Older people still speak Quechua, the Inca language; older villages and people keep Inca traditions in the form of food, music, and religious customs.)*

REVISIT THE BOOK

READER RESPONSE

1. Possible answers: Emperor: received goods, considered a god; Both: same religion, same calendar; People: gave goods to the emperor, worked in the fields
2. Answers will vary.
3. Possible responses: People are curious about the Incas. They want to see the glorious ruins of Machu Picchu.
4. Peru is located along the west coast of South America. The land is very mountainous.

EXTEND UNDERSTANDING As students look at the illustrations and photos, ask them why they like certain ones. Draw attention to the photo of a modern-day Inca farmer in the hills of Peru on page 16, and the illustration of Pizarro on page 14. Ask students to discuss in pairs how they think the ancient Incas and the Spaniards reacted to each other.

RESPONSE OPTIONS

WRITING Suggest that students write a one-paragraph journal entry from the point of view of an Inca boy or girl from ancient times. Remind them that a person's daily life depended greatly on the level of society his or her family belonged to. Ask: What tasks would your family have had? Challenge them to use descriptive details that will help a reader picture what they are describing.

MATH CONNECTION

Students can learn more about the Inca calendar by researching on the Internet or at the library. Suggest they research how the Inca used mathematics to set up their calendar.

Skill Work

TEACH/REVIEW VOCABULARY

To reinforce the contextual meaning of words like *thickets*, read the paragraph on page 3 and compare the jungle *thickets* to the high mountaintops. Continue in a similar fashion with the remaining vocabulary words.

TARGET SKILL AND STRATEGY

COMPARE AND CONTRAST Reminds students that to *compare* is to identify how two or more things are alike. To *contrast* is to identify how they are different. Explain that sometimes clue words, such as *like*, *similarly*, or *in contrast* are used. Invite students to look for clue words that signal comparisons and contrasts. As students read, have them jot down similarities and differences they identify in a Venn diagram.

VISUALIZE Remind students that to *visualize* is to create a picture in your mind as you read. Explain that this picture is often created by descriptive details, words that tell what something or someone is like. Good descriptive details help readers visualize with all five senses. Readers can imagine what something looks, smells, feels, sounds, and tastes like. Invite students, as they read, to look for descriptive details in the text that help them visualize something. Remind students that identifying descriptive details may also help them better understand compare-contrast relationships in the text.

ADDITIONAL SKILL INSTRUCTION

MAIN IDEA AND DETAILS Remind students that the *main idea* is the most important idea about a *topic*. Sometimes authors state the main idea of a paragraph or a section, but sometimes the reader must figure out the main idea for him or herself. Challenge students to answer these questions as they read: In a word or two, what (or who) is this section about? What is the most important idea about this topic? What are some details that support or tell more about the main idea?

Compare and Contrast

- To **compare** is to tell how two or more things are alike. To **contrast** is to tell how two or more things are different.
- Authors sometimes use clue words such as *similar to*, *like*, or *as* to compare things. They may use clue words such as *different from*, *but*, or *unlike* to contrast.

Directions Read the sentences below. Notice the underlined words. Circle the clue word or words that correctly show the comparison or contrast in the sentence.

1. High up in the mountains the air was clean and dry <u>like/unlike</u> the air in the steamy, damp jungle thickets.

2. The Inca government was located in the central part of the city; <u>similarly/in contrast</u>, regular citizens lived in surrounding areas.

3. Every Inca emperor built his palace in the <u>same/different</u> place: the capital city of Cuzco.

4. The walls of regular citizens' homes were made of granite; <u>similarly/however</u>, the roofs were made of grass.

5. Many Andean people worshipped the sun <u>like/unlike</u> the Incas.

6. The royal family worshipped in the magnificent temples; <u>similarly/but</u> the people took part in open-air ceremonies in the city center.

7. <u>Like/Unlike</u> other boys, the emperor's son was considered a living god.

8. The men dug holes in the ground, <u>similar to/in contrast</u> to the women, who dropped in seeds.

9. The rulers took tributes from the people, <u>as/but</u> sometimes they gave the people wages.

10. Many Andean farmers today use farming practices <u>similar to/different from</u> ones used by the ancient Incas.

Name _____

Vocabulary

Directions Choose the word from the box that best matches each definition. Write the word on the line.

Check the Words You Know
___curiosity ___glorious ___granite ___ruins
___terraced ___thickets ___torrent

1. _____ tangled jungle undergrowth

2. _____ a kind of stone

3. _____ the state of wanting to know something

4. _____ a strong current of running water

Directions Choose the word from the box that best matches each clue. Write the word on the line.

5. _____ splendid, fabulous, grand

6. _____ hard rock often used for building

7. _____ remains of ancient buildings

8. _____ leveled areas cut out of the mountainside

Directions Classify the words according to part of speech.

Nouns	Adjectives
9. _____	14. _____
10. _____	15. _____
11. _____	
12. _____	
13. _____	

Mountain Rescue

SUMMARY After yet another disagreement with her grandmother, Marisa sets off for a hike in the mountains of Grand Teton National Park with her brother Alvaro to cool off. While hiking, the pair rescues a lamb that had become trapped on a cliff. The struggle to get the lamb to safety helps Marisa realize she is not so independent after all and still needs her Abuela's help from time to time.

LESSON VOCABULARY

coil	descent	foresaw
rappel	ridge	shaft
trekked	void	

INTRODUCE THE BOOK

INTRODUCE THE TITLE AND AUTHOR Discuss the title and author of *Mountain Rescue* with students. Have students use the title and cover illustration to predict what the story might be about.

BUILD BACKGROUND Ask students if they've ever felt frustrated that a parent or other adult won't let them be as independent as they would like. Talk about their experiences and ask what they like to do to cool down when they feel frustrated. Perhaps students play sports, video games, or take long walks to help themselves feel better about things. Ask students to describe a time when they realized that the parent or other adult was right all along.

PREVIEW/USE TEXT FEATURES Ask students to look through the illustrations. Have them identify the main characters in the story. Based on the illustrations ask students what they think happens to Marisa's brother Alvaro.

ELL Point out that Marisa and Alvaro refer to their grandmother as *Abuelo,* which is the Spanish word for *grandmother.* Ask students to tell the words for *grandmother, brother, sister,* and other family members in their home languages.

READ THE BOOK

SET PURPOSE Have students set their own purpose for reading this book. The engaging illustrations may drive this purpose. As they read the book, have students imagine how Marisa and Alvaro might feel.

STRATEGY SUPPORT: STORY STRUCTURE Suggest that students track events in the story: the conflict between Marisa and Abuelo, the hike that Marisa and Alvaro take, rescuing the lamb, Alvaro's injury, and the long walk back home. Understanding this structure helps students understand the story's setting and plot.

COMPREHENSION QUESTIONS

PAGE 3 Why did Marisa argue with Abuela? *(Abuela was always worried that something bad would happen to Marisa, but Marisa wanted Abuela to trust her more.)*

PAGE 4 Why did Marisa think she should be able to go alone on the hike? *(Although Alvaro was 16, Marisa had more experience hiking, and she thought she knew more than he did.)*

PAGE 8 Where did Marisa and Al find the lamb? *(They found the lamb trapped in a small shaft in the rock about fifteen feet below the ridge where they had been hiking.)*

PAGES 16–17 Describe Marisa and Al's walk home. *(The walk home was long and difficult. Al was in pain from his fall, and Marisa was weak and dizzy from carrying the lamb on her shoulders.)*

REVISIT THE BOOK

READER RESPONSE

1. Possible response: The lamb would not have fallen down a cliff if the story was not set in the mountains; Al would not have had to climb to save the lamb; the hike back home would have been less difficult.

2. Time lines may vary, but should show the story events in order: Beginning: Marisa and Abuela argue; Marisa and Al leave on their hike. Middle: Marisa and Al find a lost lamb; Marisa rescues the lamb; Marisa carries the lamb back to Abuela's farm. End: Abuela reaches Marisa and Al; Abuela helps Marisa carry the lamb the rest of the way home.

3. *Trekked* means "made a difficult journey." Sentences will vary.

4. Responses will vary.

EXTEND UNDERSTANDING Remind students that characters are the people in a story who take part in the events. Draw attention to Marisa's actions in the story. Guide students in a discussion about what Marisa was like at the beginning of the story and how she changed by the end of the story. Have students explain the reasons for her changes.

RESPONSE OPTIONS

WRITING Suggest that students imagine that they are either Marisa or Alvaro and have them write a letter to a friend describing their adventure in the mountains of Grand Teton National Park.

SOCIAL STUDIES CONNECTION

Time For
SOCIAL
STUDIES

Invite students to use the library and the Internet to research Grand Teton National Park. Then have students work as a class to make a travel brochure about the park.

Skill Work

TEACH/REVIEW VOCABULARY

Have students look up the vocabulary words in the dictionary and write down the definitions and parts of speech. Then tell students to write a brief story that incorporates as many of the vocabulary words as possible.

TARGET SKILL AND STRATEGY

SETTING AND PLOT Remind students that the *setting* of a story is the time and place in which a story occurs. The *plot* is the pattern of events in the story. As they read the story, have them create story maps to track the events in the story. Have students think about the impact the setting of the story has on the plot. Ask: How might the story have been different in another setting?

STORY STRUCTURE Because most stories revolve around a conflict or a problem, understanding the *story structure* can help students better grasp the story. Ask students what they think the main problem of the story is. Some may think it is the arguments between Marisa and Abuleo, others may see it as the struggle Marisa and her brother had to rescue the lamb. Ask students to explain why conflict is important to the story.

ADDITIONAL SKILL INSTRUCTION

CAUSE AND EFFECT The questions *What happened?* (effect) and *Why did it happen?* (cause) help students understand *cause and effect*. Have students review the details of Alvaro's accident on page 12. Al's foot slipped as he was climbing up the rope and he twisted his arm (effect). The accident happened because the climb was difficult (cause). Have students look for other examples of cause and effect in the story.

Setting and Plot

- The **setting** is where a story takes place.
- The **plot** is an organized sequence of events.

Directions Fill in the graphic organizer below with story elements from *Mountain Rescue*.

1. Title _____

2. This story is about _____

_____
(name the characters)

_____

3. This story takes place _____

_____
(where and when)

_____

4. The action begins when _____

_____

_____

5. Then, _____

_____

_____

6. Next, _____

_____

_____

7. After that, _____

_____

_____

8. The story ends when _____

_____

_____

Name _____

Vocabulary

Directions Choose the word from the box that best matches each definition. Write the word on the line.

> ### Check the Words You Know
>
> | ___coil | ___descent | ___foresaw | ___rappel |
> |---------|-----------|-----------|-----------|
> | ___ridge | ___shaft | ___trekked | ___void |

1. climb down using a rope _____

2. empty space _____

3. something rolled up, such as a rope _____

4. process of moving down from a higher place to a lower place _____

5. traveled slowly _____

6. knew ahead of time _____

7. a deep tunnel down into the Earth _____

8. a line where two slopping surfaces meet _____

Directions Choose the word from the box that best completes each sentence. Write the word on the line.

9. Marisa pulled a _____ of rope from her backpack to tie around Al's waist.

10. Al was nervous as he began his _____ to rescue the lamb.

11. Al used the rope to _____ down to the lamb.

12. Marisa wondered if Abuelo _____ that something bad was going to happen.

Plants and Animals in Antarctica

SUMMARY Students will discover how plants and animals of Antarctica survive in such a harsh environment. They will learn the specific ways in which a variety of plants and animals have adapted to extreme conditions.

LESSON VOCABULARY

anticipation	continent
convergence	depart
forbidding	heave
icebergs	

INTRODUCE THE BOOK

INTRODUCE THE TITLE AND AUTHOR Discuss with students the title and author of *Plants and Animals in Antarctica*. Based on the title and cover illustration, ask students what they think the book is about and which plants and animals the book will include.

BUILD BACKGROUND Before reading about Antarctica, lead students to share what they already know about the topic. Many students will be familiar with whales and penguins. Ask students what special characteristics whales and penguins have. Other students may know where Antarctica is located.

PREVIEW/USE TEXT FEATURES As students preview the book, ask them if they can answer any of the questions posed in the section heads by looking at the nearest and related photograph, map, or diagram. Guide them to make predictions about what the text will be about. You may wish to record the students' predictions to discuss after reading.

ELL Guide students in looking at the photographs and section headings. Help students with difficulties they have in understanding words or picture content.

READ THE BOOK

SET PURPOSE Have students set a purpose for reading by writing five questions about plants and animals in Antarctica on their own paper. Ask students to share their questions with the class. As students read, remind them to write the answers to their questions.

STRATEGY SUPPORT: TEXT STRUCTURE As students read, model how to identify the internal text structure of a book. You may wish to review the different types of structure such as sequence, description or definition, compare and contrast, cause and effect, problem and solution, and proposition and support.

COMPREHENSION QUESTIONS

PAGE 4 Is it surprising to learn that Antarctica is considered a desert? Why? (*Responses will vary. It is surprising, because it is surrounded by oceans and covered with ice. That makes me think it would snow a lot there.*)

PAGE 5 What is the main idea of the last paragraph? Hint: It is implied. (*Antarctica is too cold for humans to live there.*)

PAGE 6 What does the word *hardy* mean in the last paragraph? (*Hardy means strong.*)

PAGE 8 Animals in Antarctica have unique features to help them survive. If you studied animals in a dry and hot desert, what could you expect to learn? (*That animals in a dry and hot climate would also need special features to survive in that type of environment.*)

PAGE 10 How do penguins' feathers help them to survive in Antarctica? (*Penguins' feathers tightly overlap to form a waterproof coat keeping the air close to their bodies warm.*)

PAGES 14–15 What text features on pages 14 and 15 can help you identify the main idea of that section? (*The section head and caption can help me identify the main idea.*)

REVISIT THE BOOK

READER RESPONSE

1. Possible response: Penguins have overlapping feathers, seals have a thick layer of blubber, and many animals eat krill to survive.
2. Possible response: The arrows clearly show how certain animals eat other animals to live.
3. Responses will vary.
4. Possible response: These small fish are important to the Antarctic food chain. If this fish becomes endangered, the food chain is affected.

EXTEND UNDERSTANDING As students read pages 6–13 about specific plants and animals in Antarctica, draw attention to the related photographs. Point out how the photographs can help them understand the facts in the text. Allow students to share their observations and comments with the class.

RESPONSE OPTIONS

WRITING Have students practice taking notes and identifying main ideas and details. Prompt students to choose their favorite section and write down the main idea first and the supporting details below.

SCIENCE CONNECTION

Discuss things that community members do that increase global warming, thereby harming the food chain in Antarctica. Students can learn more about what can be done to slow global warming by researching on the Internet or at a library. Suggest they focus on simple things their family can do to at home.

Skill Work

TEACH/REVIEW VOCABULARY

Have students identify the prefix, root, and/or suffix in each vocabulary word, if applicable.

TARGET SKILL AND STRATEGY

MAIN IDEA AND DETAILS Remind students that a *main idea* is the most important idea about a topic. Main ideas can be directly stated or implied. Explain that when main ideas are implied, students must state it in their own words. Define *supporting details* as facts that tell more about the main idea. Read the first paragraph on page 4, and ask: In a word or two what is this section about? (*Antarctica*) What is the most important idea about Antarctica? (*It is the coldest, windiest, driest, and most remote place on the Earth.*) What are some details that tell more about the main idea? (*Antarctica is surrounded by oceans.*)

TEXT STRUCTURE Recognizing *text structure* helps students identify, understand, and remember key ideas. External text structures in this book include headings, subheadings, highlighted vocabulary words, illustrations, and captions. Remind students that text features can help them to identify the main ideas and details. Lead students to identify the text features.

ADDITIONAL SKILL INSTRUCTION

GRAPHIC SOURCES Point out how *graphic sources* can assist students' comprehension before, during, and after reading. Before reading, use the graphic sources to preview and predict what the text will be about. During reading, prompt students to link the graphics to the text. After reading, clarify students' understanding by having them create their own graphic sources about what they have just read.

Main Idea and Details

- The **main idea** is the most important idea of a paragraph, passage, or book.
- Supporting **details** are facts that tell you more about the main idea.

Directions Reread the following passage from *Plants and Animals in Antarctica*. Then, answer the questions below.

> Antarctica has two seasons: A very long, dark winter and a very short, bright summer. In winter, you may see days with just one hour of sunlight.
>
> Blizzards happen in Antarctica when raging winds blow snow along the surface. Surface winds can sweep up loose snow at more than 100 miles an hour. These winds cause severe blizzard conditions that may last a week or longer.
>
> You wouldn't want to live in Antarctica. But then again, you probably couldn't live there. It's simply too cold and forbidding.

1. What is the passage about? (State your answer in two words.)

_____

2. What is the main idea of the passage?

_____

_____

_____

3. What three details support the main idea?

   1) _____

   _____

   2) _____

   _____

   3) _____

   _____

Name _____

Vocabulary

Directions Synonyms are words that have the same meaning. Draw a line to match the synonyms.

> ## Check the Words You Know
>
> ___anticipation ___continent ___convergence ___depart
> ___forbidding ___heave ___icebergs

1. anticipation   **a.** meeting

2. convergence   **b.** lift

3. depart   **c.** leave

4. forbidding   **d.** unfriendly

5. heave   **e.** expectation

Directions Write five sentences using one vocabulary word in each sentence.

6. _____

_____

7. _____

_____

8. _____

_____

9. _____

_____

10. _____

_____

Stuart's Moon Suit

SUMMARY Stuart creates a moon suit costume with the same components of the space suit worn by Neil Armstrong when he walked on the Moon. Along the way, Stuart learns about the functions of a space suit.

LESSON VOCABULARY

loomed	rille
runt	staggered
summoning	taunted
trench	trudged

INTRODUCE THE BOOK

INTRODUCE THE TITLE AND AUTHOR Discuss with students the title and the author of *Stuart's Moon Suit*. Based on the title and the cover illustration, ask students if they think this is a fiction or nonfiction book. Why? What do they think this book will be about?

BUILD BACKGROUND Ask students to share what they know about flights to the moon. Ask why astronauts have to wear special suits. What else do astronauts have to do to prepare? Invite students to share what they know about the moon and space.

PREVIEW/USE TEXT FEATURES Have students look at the illustrations in the book. Ask who is the main character in the book. What does Stuart seem to be assembling? Have students look at page 14. Ask: How might a space suit provide protection in this type of environment?

READ THE BOOK

SET PURPOSE Have students set a purpose for reading *Stuart's Moon Suit*. Their curiosity about how Stuart can make a moon suit may drive this purpose. Encourage students to say how they would prepare to travel to the Moon.

STRATEGY SUPPORT: MONITOR AND FIX UP As students read, encourage them to self-question to monitor their comprehension and to practice fix up strategies. Invite them to look at the illustrations if they are having difficulty picturing the details of the space suit. You may pause every few pages for students to talk with a partner about what they have read.

COMPREHENSION QUESTIONS

PAGE 5 What conclusion did Stuart come to about Space Travel Day? *(He decided to be Neil Armstrong.)*

PAGE 8 What role does Doris play in the story? *(She asks a lot of questions that Stuart has to answer, also, she's skeptical and so Stuart shows her that he knows what he's doing.)*

PAGES 12–13 What is the ITMG? What does it do? *(Integrated Thermal Micrometeoroid Garment. Protects astronaut from extreme temperatures.)*

PAGE 18 What do you think of Stuart's moon suit? *(Answers will vary.)*

PAGE 20 What is the main idea? What are some supporting details? *(Apollo 11 landed on the Moon in 1969. People around world watched on TV. Armstrong and Aldrin took photos, collected rock and soil samples.)*

ELL Have English language learners work in pairs to retell *Stuart's Moon Suit* in their own words. Encourage students to use the pictures in the book as prompts as they retell the story.

REVISIT THE BOOK

READER RESPONSE

1. Possible response: Stuart's suit had models of the components in Armstrong's suit. It couldn't do the actual things Armstrong's suit did.
2. Responses will vary.
3. *Rile*—to make someone angry; *rill*—a stream. Sentences will vary but should demonstrate understanding of the words.
4. Responses will vary.

EXTEND UNDERSTANDING Invite students to look at the NASA web site for a view of a real space suit. How has reading *Stuart's Moon Suit* helped students better understand how a space suit works?

RESPONSE OPTIONS

WRITING Invite students to imagine a walk on the moon. Have them consider Stuart's description of the atmosphere on the moon and write a journal entry about their walk.

SCIENCE CONNECTION

TIME FOR Science

Have students choose another moon or planet in our solar system to research and report on.

Skill Work

TEACH/REVIEW VOCABULARY

Pair students and assign each partner four vocabulary words. Have students find their words in the story, write definitions based on context clues, and write a sentence for each word showing its meaning. Have partners share their definitions with the class. Encourage students to discuss any differences in their definitions.

TARGET SKILL AND STRATEGY

DRAW CONCLUSIONS Explain: When you *draw conclusions*, you use what you know about a story to make decisions about facts and details. Have students read pages 4 and 5. Ask: Is Stuart really interested in Neil Armstrong? What makes you think so? *(He knows all about him; he's eager to make a space suit.)* Have students read page 6. Ask what conclusions they can draw about Stuart. *(He's interested in space travel and in Neil Armstrong. He pays attention to details. He's excited about his project.)*

MONITOR AND FIX UP Remind students that good readers constantly *monitor* themselves to make sure they understand what they are reading. When comprehension falters, they use *fix-up* strategies (adjusting their reading rate, reading on, rereading and reviewing, seeking help from others). As students read pages 8–12, have them ask themselves questions to assess their understanding. *(What happens first? What is this part about?)* Review what they learned about Stuart's space suit in this section.

ADDITIONAL SKILL INSTRUCTION

MAIN IDEA AND DETAILS Remind students that the *main idea* is the most important idea about a topic. *Supporting details* are small pieces of information that tell more about the main idea. Point out that sometimes the main idea will be clearly stated, but sometimes readers will have to figure it out for themselves. Have students try to state the main idea of the selection and point out supporting details after reading.

Draw Conclusions

Draw conclusions is to use what you know about whatever you're reading to make decisions about facts and details in the text.

Directions Create a concept map about Neil Armstrong's space suit. Think of the categories you want to use. Then write a category in each circle. Fill in the details you learned under the appropriate category. How does each piece work with the atmosphere of the moon?

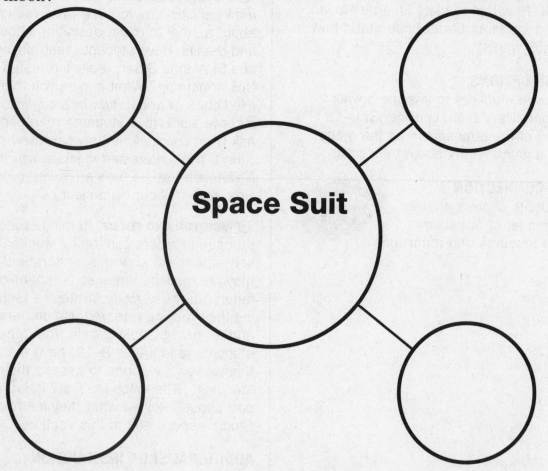

Space Suit

Directions Write your response to this question: Did Stuart do a good job creating a space suit like Neil Armstrong's? Why or why not?

_____

_____

_____

_____

Vocabulary

Directions Choose the word from the box that best matches each definition.
Write the word on the line.

Check the Words You Know

___loomed	___rille	___runt	___staggered
___summoning	___taunted	___trench	___trudged

---

1. _____ a long, narrow trench on the moon

2. _____ felt threatening or foreboding

3. _____ walked slowly and with effort, plodded

4. _____ tried to upset someone by teasing

5. _____ a small person; the smallest animal in a litter

6. _____ walked unsteadily

7. _____ a ditch

8. _____ calling someone or something to come

Directions Write the word from the box that completes each sentence.

9. Andy _____ to class on the day of the test.

10. "Dinner's ready," said her father, _____ her to the house.

11. Our puppy was the _____ of the litter.

12. The thought of the long drive to the ocean _____ in my mind.

13. A _____ ran along the side of the highway.

14. She _____ across the finish line at the end of her race.

15. We could see the _____ in the photograph of the moon.

16. Joe often _____ his little brother.

We Shall Overcome

SUMMARY This book looks at those who fought for Civil Rights in America and why. It begins with the abolitionists who worked to end slavery in the 1800s and ends with the Civil Rights movement of the 1950s and 1960s.

LESSON VOCABULARY

ancestors	avoided
generations	minister
numerous	pulpit
shielding	

INTRODUCE THE BOOK

INTRODUCE THE TITLE AND AUTHOR Discuss with students the title and the author of *We Shall Overcome*. Ask students to describe the photograph on the front cover. Ask students where they think the title for this book comes from. Based on the title, what information do they think this book will provide?

BUILD BACKGROUND Ask students to share what they know about the history of slavery in the United States. Point out that the end of slavery didn't bring equal rights for African Americans. Ask students what the term "equal rights" means. Ask them to name people who have fought for equal rights in America.

PREVIEW/USE TEXT FEATURES Ask students to look at the photographs, captions, and headings in the book. Ask if any faces or names are familiar to them. Do students notice anything about the progression of the photos? Ask: Do you think this book covers a series of events in history? Why do you think so?

READ THE BOOK

SET PURPOSE Have students set a purpose for reading *We Shall Overcome*. Their interest in the Civil Rights movement and its causes and effects may guide this purpose. You may encourage them to look for cause-and-effect relationships throughout the book as they read. Ask students to think about why the struggle for equal rights was deeper and more personal for African Americans.

STRATEGY SUPPORT: ANSWER QUESTIONS Encourage students to use QAR (question-answer relationships) to pose questions as they read to help identify the causes and effects of slavery and the civil rights movement. Most of the questions that they ask should be "Think and Search" or "Author and Me" (text plus prior knowledge).

COMPREHENSION QUESTIONS

PAGE 3 What was one of the causes of slavery in the United States? What were its effects? *(Possible response: Cause: Needed workers for plantations. Effects: African Americans have struggled for generations to be treated as equals.)*

PAGES 6–9 Name two abolitionists and what they did. *(Possible response: David Walker told enslaved people to use force when rebelling. Maria Stewart wrote and made speeches about making African Americans' lives better.)*

PAGES 12–13 What two decisions did the Supreme Court make in the 1950s? *(Black students couldn't be prevented from attending school with white students; It was unconstitutional to separate people on buses.)*

PAGE 19 What does the last sentence of the book mean? *(Possible response: Knowing about the people in history who have fought for equal rights gives people today strength to keep trying to overcome prejudice.)*

REVISIT THE BOOK

READER RESPONSE

1. Possible response: Cause: Harriet Tubman escaped to freedom. Effect: She became a well-known conductor of the Underground Railroad. Cause: Rosa Parks wouldn't give up her bus seat for a white person. Effect: Black people boycotted buses; the Supreme Court made it illegal to force black people to sit in the backs of buses.
2. Baumfree felt that since she had a new life, she should have a new name. Responses to other questions will vary.
3. *avoids, avoiding, avoidable, unavoidable*
4. Sojourner Truth, Harriet Tubman, Rosa Parks

EXTEND UNDERSTANDING Have students look at the photos on pages 3–4. Ask students to describe what they see and what they feel when they look at these photos. Ask: How do these photos give greater depth to the material you just read in the text?

RESPONSE OPTIONS

WRITING Ask students to pretend they are abolitionists or civil rights workers. Have them write newspaper editorials to the paper that support their views and try to persuade others to join their fight.

SOCIAL STUDIES CONNECTION

Time For SOCIAL STUDIES

Encourage students to find out more about famous African Americans in United States history—inventors, teachers, doctors, politicians, and so on. Have students choose how to present their findings (time line, collage, or report) and encourage them to include archival pictures and photos.

Skill Work

TEACH/REVIEW VOCABULARY

Have students write the vocabulary words and their definitions on separate index cards. Ask students to put the words into groups of nouns (people, place, or thing), verbs (action words), and adjectives (describing words).

ELL Have students work in pairs with more proficient speakers to complete the vocabulary activity above.

TARGET SKILL AND STRATEGY

CAUSE AND EFFECT Remind students that a *cause* means why something happened, and an *effect* is what happened. To help students practice identifying cause-and-effect relationships, have them read page 11. Ask: Why did Lincoln sign the Emancipation Proclamation in 1863? *(He wanted to end slavery.)* What was the Proclamation's effect? *(Some enslaved people were freed.)*

ANSWER QUESTIONS Point out that *answering questions* means providing complete and focused responses and that it can help students learn from their reading. Remind students about the different types of questions they may encounter, such as "Right There," "On My Own," and "Think and Search." Most questions before and during reading will be one of these three. Have students read pages 3–5 and identify which type of question you ask. Ask: What do you know about slavery in the United States? *(On My Own)* Where did the first captured Africans work when they came to America? *(Right There)* How did captured Africans and abolitionists fight against slavery? *(Think and Search)*

ADDITIONAL SKILL INSTRUCTION

SEQUENCE Remind students that keeping track of a *sequence of events*, or the order in which they happen, can help them better understand historical information. To practice identifying events in a sequence, have students read pages 12–13. Together make a sequential list of the important events from those pages.

Cause and Effect

- The **cause** is why something happened, and the **effect** is what happened.
- A single cause may have more than one effect.

Directions Complete the graphic organizer below by writing effects of the cause that is given. Then answer the question below.

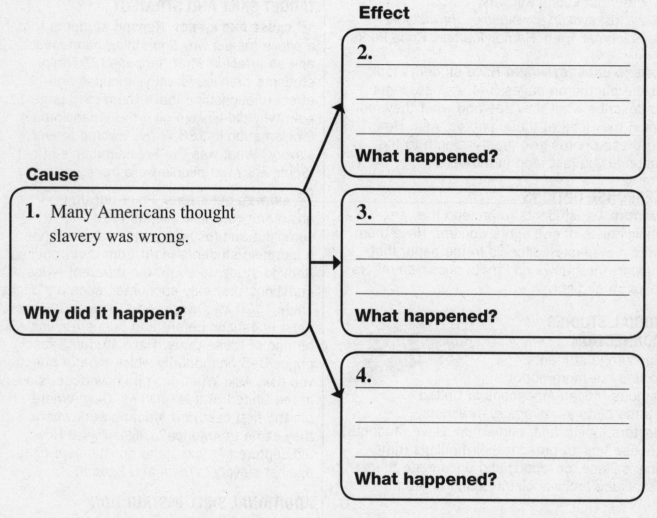

Effect

2. _____

_____

_____

What happened?

Cause

1. Many Americans thought slavery was wrong.

Why did it happen?

3. _____

_____

_____

What happened?

4. _____

_____

_____

What happened?

5. How did the actions of the Abolitionist Movement bring about change? What was the effect on the United States?

_____

_____

_____

_____

Name _____

Vocabulary

Directions For each word, write the letter of its definition.

```
┌─────────────────────────────────────────────┐
│         Check the Words You Know            │
│  ┌───────────────────────────────────────┐  │
│  │ ___ ancestors      ___ avoided        │  │
│  │ ___ generations    ___ minister       │  │
│  │ ___ numerous       ___ pulpit         │  │
│  │ ___ shielding                         │  │
│  └───────────────────────────────────────┘  │
└─────────────────────────────────────────────┘
```

_____ 1. pulpit

_____ 2. shielding

_____ 3. avoided

_____ 4. minister

_____ 5. ancestors

_____ 6. numerous

a. pastor

b. great-grandparents

c. many

d. stayed away

e. protecting

f. platform

Directions Choose the word from the box that best completes each sentence.

7. In the United States, _____ of African Americans have worked for

   equal rights.

8. Conductors on the Underground Railroad worked hard _____ the

   runaways from danger.

9. The African American students who sat at lunch counters waiting to be served

   _____ using violence to get what they wanted.

10. Reverend Dr. Martin Luther King, Jr. was a _____ and leader of the

    Civil Rights Movement.

SUMMARY This book gives students some background information about the Native American heritage of athlete Jim Thorpe. Students will learn about the history of the Sauk and Fox tribes and their way of life.

LESSON VOCABULARY

boarding schools	dormitory
endurance	manual
reservation	society

INTRODUCE THE BOOK

INTRODUCE THE TITLE AND AUTHOR Discuss with students the title and the author of *The Sauk and Fox: Native Americans*. Direct students' attention to the triangle labeled "Social Studies" and ask students how they think this book relates to social studies.

BUILD BACKGROUND Discuss with students what they know about the history and the treatment of Native Americans in our country.

PREVIEW/USE TEXT FEATURES Suggest that students preview the photographs and illustrations in this book. Ask students what details they can pick up about the Native American culture from these features.

READ THE BOOK

SET PURPOSE Have students *set a purpose* for reading *The Sauk and Fox*. Students' interest and curiosity about Native Americans and about Jim Thorpe should guide this purpose.

STRATEGY SUPPORT: SUMMARIZE Remind students that *summarizing* a story can also help them determine the author's purpose. Have them sum up the story in two or three sentences. Ask them to add a statement about the author's purpose.

COMPREHENSION QUESTIONS

PAGE 5 Is it a statement of fact or a statement of opinion that many Native Americans were poor? *(fact)*

PAGE 6 What do the Sauk and Fox tribes teach us about cooperation? *(Different groups of people can live side by side and become a community.)*

PAGE 12 How does the description of Sauk and Fox women help you understand how they played important roles in their community? *(They made clothing, took care of other mothers, and farmed—all important jobs in the community.)*

PAGE 18 How could Jim Thorpe's success in the Olympics help give the Native Americans courage? *(They might feel that if one Native American can succeed against the odds, so can others.)*

REVIST THE BOOK

READER RESPONSE

1. Possible responses: Fact: Men were chiefs. Opinion: Peace chiefs were kind and fair.

2. Possible response: In the 1600s and 1700s, two similar Native American tribes, the Sauk and Fox, lived in the Midwest. The U.S. government wanted their lands, so they sent the tribes to live in smaller areas and tried to change the way they lived. But when Jim Thorpe, a fellow Native American, was successful in the Olympic games, it strengthened the pride of all Native Americans and gave them the courage to hold onto their traditions.

3. Possible response: a place on an airplane or in a restaurant that someone has asked to be held for him or her. Sentences will vary.

4. Possible responses: The Sauk and Fox were farmers. They lived in long, loaf-shaped houses. They hunted with bows and arrows.

EXTEND UNDERSTANDING Invite students to look at the illustration on page 6. Ask students to describe what is going on in this illustration. Then ask students how this illustration gives them important visual clues to how the Sauk and Fox nations got along together so well.

RESPONSE OPTIONS

WRITING Ask students to imagine that they are young members of either the Sauk or the Fox Native American tribe. Suggest that they write letters to someone they know, describing how Jim Thorpe's success in the Olympic games makes them feel proud and excited.

SOCIAL STUDIES CONNECTION

Invite students to research another Native American tribe and to present their reports to the class.

Time For SOCIAL STUDIES

Skill Work

TEACH/REVIEW VOCABULARY

Make a word-search puzzle that contains all of the vocabulary words. After students have circled the words, prompt them to write the meaning of each word.

ELL Review the vocabulary with students. Then give students a vocabulary word and multiple definitions for it. Direct students how to choose the correct one. Repeat this process with the remaining vocabulary words.

TARGET SKILL AND STRATEGY

FACT AND OPINION Remind students that a *statement of fact* tells something that can be proved true or false by reading, observing, or asking an expert. A *statement of opinion* tells someone's ideas or feelings and cannot be proved. Remind students that some sentences contain both statements of fact and statements of opinion. Give students a series of statements of fact and statements of opinion. Prompt them to identify the statements of fact with an *F* and the statements of opinion with an *O*.

SUMMARIZE Remind students that *summarizing*, or retelling the important information in the book, can help them remember the sequence of events. Ask: How does summarizing help you better understand the history of Sauk and Fox Native American tribes?

ADDITIONAL SKILL INSTRUCTION

PLOT AND THEME Remind students that *plot* organizes events to move the story forward. As students read, they should identify the most important events. Remind students that the *theme* is the big idea of the story and that knowing the plot can help them determine the theme. Review with students the plot and theme of a story recently read by the group. Then help them identify the plot and theme of this reading selection.

Fact and Opinion

- A **statement of fact** is a statement that can be proved or disproved.
- A **statement of opinion** cannot be proved.

1. Write a fact about yourself.

_____

_____

2. Now write an opinion about yourself.

_____

_____

3. Write a fact about your hair.

_____

_____

4. Now write an opinion about your hair.

_____

_____

5. Write a fact about your favorite TV show.

_____

_____

6. Now write an opinion about your favorite TV show.

_____

_____

7. Write a fact about *The Sauk and Fox*.

_____

_____

8. Now write an opinion.

_____

_____

Name _____

Vocabulary

Directions Choose the word from the box that best completes each sentence.

Check the Words You Know
___boarding schools   ___dormitory
___endurance   ___manual
___reservation   ___society

1. The Native Americans lived on a _____.

2. At _____, students lived in buildings with many other children.

3. At the school, the girls slept in a _____.

4. This car doesn't have an automatic shift, but a _____ one.

5. You have to have a great deal of _____ to lift such heavy weights for such a long time.

6. In the Native Americans' _____, the men hunted and the women farmed.

Directions Write a short paragraph about what life was like for the Sauk and Fox after they moved to the reservations. Use as many vocabulary words as you can.

_____

_____

_____

_____

_____

_____

_____

_____

Living With Grandpa Joseph

SUMMARY This story is about a family who invites their grandfather to live with them while he recuperates from a hip injury. At first it looks as though it will be difficult, because they don't really have enough room. But soon everyone is glad to have Grandpa Joseph around. He tells twins Annie and Kevin stories about the war and shows interest in Kevin's flute playing. In the end, the experience of having their grandfather stay with them draws the family closer together.

LESSON VOCABULARY

affords	colonel
glint	lurking
palette	quaint
resemblance	

INTRODUCE THE BOOK

INTRODUCE THE TITLE AND AUTHOR Discuss with students the title and the author of *Living With Grandpa Joseph*. Based on the title, ask students what kind of information they think this book will provide. Direct students to look at the cover illustration to see if they can get more clues about the story's content.

BUILD BACKGROUND Ask students to talk about their grandparents and discuss what it would be like to have them visit for a long time. What sorts of things do they enjoy doing with their grandparents? Do their grandparents have any hobbies? What interests do students share with their grandparents?

PREVIEW/USE TEXT FEATURES Invite students to look at all the illustrations in the book. Ask students how the illustrations give clues as to what is going to happen in the story.

READ THE BOOK

SET PURPOSE Have students set a purpose for reading *Living With Grandpa Joseph*. Their interest in their own grandparents can guide this purpose.

STRATEGY SUPPORT: INFERRING Remind students that when they *infer*, they use information from the story and what they already know to come up with their own ideas. Illustrations and a character's actions in a story can help readers make inferences about the character.

COMPREHENSION QUESTIONS

PAGES 4–5 Why does Grandpa Joseph have to come and stay with his daughter and her family? (*He broke his hip and needs to take it easy while he recovers.*)

PAGE 5 When did Grandpa Joseph's wife die? (*three years ago*)

PAGE 9 What is Grandpa Joseph's one hobby that he still can do, despite his broken hip? (*paint*)

PAGES 10–11 What stories do Annie and Kevin most like to hear their grandpa tell? (*stories about the war*)

PAGE 19 What does Grandpa decide to paint at the end of the story? (*a portrait of the whole family*)

REVISIT THE BOOK

READER RESPONSE

1. Possible response: The family had to clean out the computer room. Grandpa Joseph had to pack up his belongings. The kids couldn't watch TV or use the computer as much as they used to.
2. Responses will vary.
3. Possible response: a board for mixing paint
4. Possible response: They like Grandpa's stories; they like the interest he takes in them.

EXTEND UNDERSTANDING Discuss with students how chapters in books can help organize complicated material. Go over the story's four chapters with students. Discuss what material is in each chapter. Ask students to explain how they can tell what each chapter is going to be about and to explain how each chapter is a progression from the last one.

RESPONSE OPTIONS

WRITING Have students imagine that one of their grandparents has to come and live with them for a month. Have them describe where the grandparent would stay and what they would do together. What interests do the students and grandparents share?

SOCIAL STUDIES CONNECTION

Time For SOCIAL STUDIES

Have students research the Rocky Mountains. How many large cities are located in or near the Rocky Mountains? What can you do on a vacation to the Rocky Mountains? Use the library to find out more.

Skill Work

TEACH/REVIEW VOCABULARY

Encourage student pairs to find the vocabulary words in the text. Have them define the words and work together to write a sentence for each word.

ELL Ask students to skim the story and write down any unfamiliar words. Suggest that they look up the words in a dictionary and write the meanings in their notebooks.

TARGET SKILL AND STRATEGY

SEQUENCE Remind students that the *sequence* is the order of events in a story. Each event leads to another event. As students read *Living With Grandpa Joseph*, have them pay attention to what happens *first*, *next*, and *last*.

INFERRING Remind students that to *infer*, you combine what you know with text clues to come up with your own ideas. Have students infer one thing about Grandpa Joseph. Ask: How did the text clues and your own experiences help you infer this?

ADDITIONAL SKILL INSTRUCTION

CHARACTER Explain that *characters* are the people or animals in a story. Authors let us know what characters are like by telling us their thoughts, actions, or reactions to others. As students read the selection, remind them to look for clues to what the characters are like. Have them use a graphic organizer to record their notes.

Sequence

- **Sequence** is the order of events in a story.

Directions Put the following events from *Living with Grandpa Joseph* in the correct sequence by writing 1–10 on the lines.

_____ **1.** Kevin and Annie helped their parents get the computer room ready for Grandpa Joseph.

_____ **2.** As he told the story, Annie sat at his feet to hear better.

_____ **3.** Mom and the children rushed to the hospital.

_____ **4.** Grandpa Joseph watched the sun rise over the Rocky Mountains.

_____ **5.** The family drove to the hospital to pick up Grandpa.

_____ **6.** Grandpa tried to help out with dinner.

_____ **7.** They all shared a memory of Grandpa Joseph.

_____ **8.** "I feel like painting today!" Grandpa Joseph said.

_____ **9.** The doctor had a different idea.

_____ **10.** The bowl fell out of his hands and onto the floor.

Name _____

Vocabulary

Directions Complete each sentence with a word from the box.

Check the Words You Know

__affords	__colonel	__glint	__lurking
__palette	__quaint	__resemblance	

---

1. Annie bore a striking _____ to her mother.

2. When Grandpa fought in the war, he was promoted all the way to

   _____.

3. Just thinking about playing for Grandpa gave Kevin a _____ in his eye.

4. Grandpa's window _____ a stunning view of the Rockies.

5. When Grandpa painted with his watercolors, he used a _____ for his paints.

6. Grandpa and Grandma used to live in a _____ white house on a quiet street.

7. The children couldn't get enough of their Grandpa, and spent hours

   _____ around his room.

Directions Write a brief paragraph discussing Grandpa Joseph using as many vocabulary words as possible.

_____

_____

_____

_____

_____

_____

_____

To Be a Star

SUMMARY In this realistic fiction selection, Becky wins the lead part in a play. Although she memorizes her lines, she becomes frustrated when she cannot read with expression and feeling. After talking with her grandpa, Becky comes up with a plan to save the school play.

LESSON VOCABULARY

abundance	backdrop
ceremonial	drought
graze	shock

INTRODUCE THE BOOK

INTRODUCE THE TITLE AND AUTHOR Discuss the title and author of *To Be a Star*. Based on the title and the illustration on the cover, ask students to predict what they think this story might be about. Ask students to point out the star of the play. Discuss with them the roles of the other actors in a play.

BUILD BACKGROUND Ask students to talk about plays they have been part of or have seen. Discuss what it takes to put on a play, such as directing, acting, painting the set, and working the lights and sound. Point out that it takes lots of people working together to put on a play.

PREVIEW/USE TEXT FEATURES Invite students to look at the illustrations in the book. Ask students how the illustrations give clues to what might happen in the story. Have students describe the picture of the students on page 15. Ask: What are the students doing? What clues helped you figure it out? Why do you think one student looks nervous? What might she be worried about?

READ THE BOOK

SET PURPOSE Have students set a purpose for reading *To Be a Star*. Ask them to look at the cover and use the illustration as clues to the mood of the story. Ask: How do you think the characters feel? Why do you think they feel this way?

STRATEGY SUPPORT: PREDICT AND SET PURPOSE As they read, have students *set a purpose* for reading by encouraging them to think about the purpose of a fictional story. (to entertain) Have them look at the photo on page 20 and think about how this page relates to the rest of the story.

COMPREHENSION QUESTIONS

PAGE 3 Based on the pictures on the cover and on page 3, how are the settings different from one another? *(Possible responses: The play on the cover takes place long ago. I can tell by the way the characters are dressed. I think the time and place might be the first Thanksgiving. The picture on page 3 takes place now. The teacher and the students dress like we do today.)*

PAGE 5 How do you know that Marta is a good friend? *(Possible responses: Although she did not get the lead part in the play, Marta is still happy for Becky and says that it will be fun for both of them to act together in the play.)*

PAGES 9–10 What generalization can you make about Becky's dad? What facts support your answer? *(Possible responses: Becky's dad is silly, fun, and caring. He wants to help Becky with her lines in the play. He dresses up in and old scarf and sweater and reads the lines in a squeaky voice and uses exaggerated gestures to make her laugh.)*

PAGES 13–14 What do you predict will happen next? *(Possible answer: Becky will listen to her grandpa's advice and ask for a smaller part in the play.)*

PAGES 17–19 Was your prediction accurate? Was there anything you did not expect to happen? Explain. *(Possible responses: I predicted that Becky would take a smaller part in the play and I was correct. I didn't expect that she would switch parts with Marta.)*

REVISIT THE BOOK

READER RESPONSE

1. Possible responses: Everyone in Becky's family helps her with the play; Becky's mom practices with her and gives helpful suggestions; Becky's dad wears a costume and reads lines; Becky's grandpa gives her suggestions and tells her how he learned to act

2. Possible responses: He says that being a star is doing what is best for the play and Becky begins to think about what he said. Becky decides it would be better to switch parts with Marta. I think Becky will do more acting after this play because she felt more comfortable; I think she will take smaller parts until she gains confidence. Becky before the play: nervous about performing; wants to be a star; frustrated with her performance. Becky after the play; isn't nervous; knows what it means to be a star; is no longer frustrated

3. Possible responses: Backdrop means "background." The story says that Becky stood against the painted backdrop. In the picture, Becky and the others are standing on stage in front of the painted background. I took a picture of Mom against a backdrop of red roses.

4. Possible responses: I think I would have been nervous just like Becky. I probably would have made the same choice as Becky. I would want someone else to have a chance to play the main part and taking a less important part would make me less nervous.

EXTEND UNDERSTANDING Discuss with students that plays are divided into acts and scenes. Point out that an act has many different scenes and that acts usually have breaks in between them. Tell students to think of acts as chapters in a book and scenes as paragraphs or sections in that chapter.

RESPONSE OPTIONS

SPEAKING AND WRITING Invite pairs to write a short scene for Becky and Marta to perform as the characters Sara and Mary for their school Thanksgiving play.

DRAMA CONNECTION

Have pairs rehearse the scenes they wrote for Becky and Marta. Then have students perform their scenes for the group. Remind students to use gestures, maintain eye contact, and read with expression.

Skill Work

TEACH/REVIEW VOCABULARY

Have students look up the vocabulary words in the dictionary and write down the definitions. Then tell students to write a brief story using all the vocabulary words.

ELL Have pairs skim the story together and write down unfamiliar words. Point out that they should also write down words that they think they know but of which they cannot recall the meaning. Tell them to look up the words in a dictionary and write down the meanings. Then have them use each word in a meaningful sentence.

TARGET SKILL AND STRATEGY

GENERALIZE Point out that authors may present ideas about several things or people and then make a general statement about all of them together. This statement is called a *generalization*. Clue words such as *most*, *all*, *always*, and *never* help identify generalizations. Valid generalizations are accurate because they are based on facts, while faulty generalizations are not.

PREDICT AND SET PURPOSE Remind students that when they set a *purpose* for reading, they are deciding what their reason will be for reading a selection. To *predict* means to tell what you think might happen next. Explain that when they predict the outcome of a story, they are setting a purpose for reading.

ADDITIONAL SKILL INSTRUCTION

SETTING Remind students that the setting is the time and place in which a story takes place. As students read, have them ask themselves: Where is this scene taking place? Does this part of the story seem to be taking place in the past, the present, or the future?

Generalize

Directions Complete the chart with facts from the story that support the generalization.

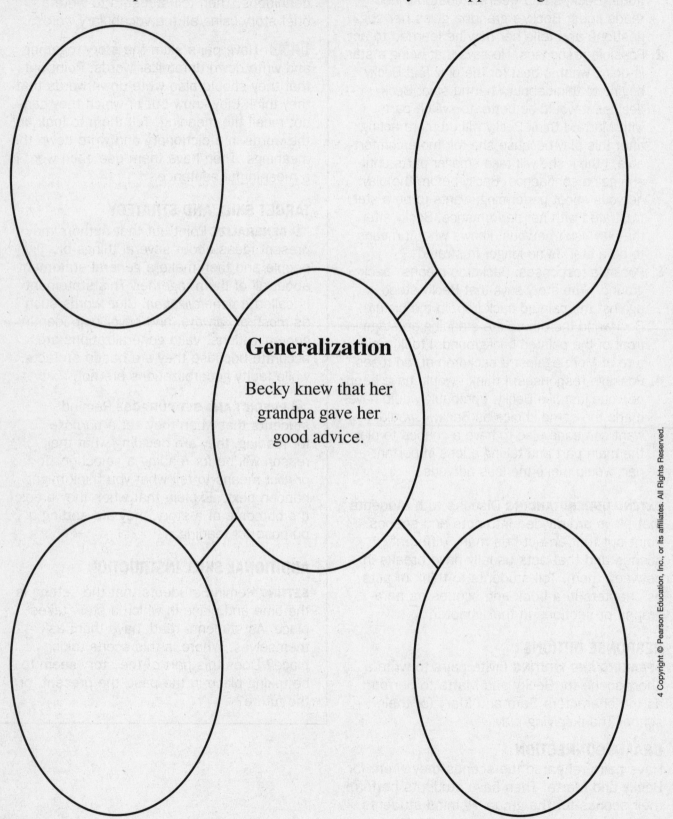

Generalization

Becky knew that her grandpa gave her good advice.

Vocabulary

Directions Write each vocabulary word next to its definition below.

Check the Words You Know

___abundance   ___backdrop   ___ceremonial
___drought   ___graze   ___shock

1. _____ formal

2. _____ to feed on growing grass

3. _____ surprise

4. _____ plentiful; overflowing

5. _____ long, dry spell

6. _____ background

Directions Choose three words and use each word in a sentence.

7. _____

_____

8. _____

_____

9. _____

_____

Earth's Closest Neighbor

SUMMARY *Earth's Closest Neighbor* explains the characteristics and phases of Earth's natural satellite. The nonfiction book also describes efforts by people to explore the moon.

LESSON VOCABULARY

astronauts	capsule
hatch	horizon
lunar	module
quarantine	

INTRODUCE THE BOOK

INTRODUCE THE TITLE AND AUTHOR Discuss with students the title and the author of *Earth's Closest Neighbor*. Point out the genre, content triangle, and content category on the cover. Discuss with students what they expect the book to be about.

BUILD BACKGROUND Invite volunteers to tell what they know about the moon. Talk about the different ways the moon appears in the sky. Ask students what they know about people's attempts to reach the moon and explore its surface.

PREVIEW/USE TEXT FEATURES Have students skim through the book, looking at the headings, pictures, and captions. Ask: Do you see anything about the moon in these pages that is familiar to you? *(Possible responses: moon orbiting Earth, pictures of the phases of the moon, eclipses, rockets, astronauts)* Discuss how the book is organized into sections and what students expect to learn from each section based on the headings.

READ THE BOOK

SET PURPOSE Have students set their own purposes for reading by completing one of the following two statements: "What I want to learn about the moon is _____" or "What I want to learn about visiting the moon is _____."

STRATEGY SUPPORT: BACKGROUND KNOWLEDGE To activate background knowledge, have students brainstorm what information they already know about the moon. Students should write that information on a concept web on the board.

COMPREHENSION QUESTIONS

PAGE 4 What is the main idea of the first paragraph on this page? *(Possible response: The moon is Earth's only natural satellite.)*

PAGE 7 How does the graphic source on this page help you understand the phases of the moon? *(Possible response: It shows what the phases look like, so I understand the descriptions of the phases better.)*

PAGE 16 Monitor your reading of this page. What fix-up strategy did you use, if any? *(Possible response: I do not understand the parts of the Apollo 11 spacecraft. I'm going to read on to see if there's more information about it.)*

PAGE 18 How do the graphic sources on this page help you understand the text? *(Possible response: They help me visualize the parts of the Apollo 11 spacecraft that I found confusing.)*

REVISIT THE BOOK

READER RESPONSE

1. Possible response: It helped me identify the size and shape of the moon in its various stages as it orbits Earth.

2. Responses will vary.

3. Possible responses: a trapdoor covering an opening in an aircraft; to come out of an egg

4. Responses may include any of the following in order: Oct. 4, 1957: Soviets launch *Sputnik 1*; Oct. 1, 1958: NASA is formed; April 12, 1961: Soviet astronaut completes one orbit of Earth; May 25, 1961: Kennedy announces goal of landing an astronaut on the moon by the end of the decade; February 20, 1962: John Glenn Jr. orbits Earth; June 3, 1965: Edward H. White II becomes the first U.S. astronaut to conduct a space walk.

EXTEND UNDERSTANDING Point out that authors of nonfiction books often use headings to divide and group information into sections. The information in each section usually relates to the same topic, and the heading may even alert the reader to the main idea.

RESPONSE OPTIONS

VIEWING Show students a film or video about the first moon landing. At the end of the movie, have students describe any new information about the moon or *Apollo 11* that they learned from the film. Discuss how seeing footage of the moon landing furthers their understanding of the information in *Earth's Closest Neighbor*.

SCIENCE CONNECTION

TIME FOR Science

Explain to students that while Earth has a gravitational pull on the moon, the moon also has its own effect on Earth. Have students research what effects the moon has on Earth, including the tides and magnetic fields. Students may also try to find legends, myths, and superstitions that people have had about the moon's effects on people. Invite them to research any scientific support or denial of these claims.

Skill Work

TEACH/REVIEW VOCABULARY

Divide the class into groups and assign one vocabulary word to each group. Have each group create a word web with clues for its word, leaving the center blank. Clues may include the definition, part of speech, synonyms or antonyms. Have groups exchange webs and guess the words.

TARGET SKILL AND STRATEGY

GRAPHIC FEATURES Review with students that *graphic features* are visual aids (pictures with captions, time lines, graphs, and maps) intended to help the reader understand information in a book. As they read, have students think about how the graphic features help them understand the information in the book.

BACKGROUND KNOWLEDGE Explain to students that *background knowledge*, either from personal experience or books, is what they already know about a topic. Point out that using their background knowledge can help them better understand the information in a story. Have students tell how their background knowledge helped them as they read.

ADDITIONAL SKILL INSTRUCTION

MAIN IDEA AND DETAILS Remind students that the *main idea* of a passage in a book is the most important idea. *Supporting details* are the smaller pieces of information that tell more about the main idea. Point out that often the main idea of a section of a book can be found in a sentence or in the heading of the passage. For each section of the book, have students write down the main idea and two supporting details.

ELL Invite students to share any myths about the moon that are popular in their cultures.

Graphic Features

- **Graphic features** are visual aids such as illustrations, photographs with captions, graphs, and time lines.

Directions Answer the following questions using using information from *Earth's Closest Neighbor*.

1. Look at the graphic features again on page 4 of the book. How does the bottom picture help you understand the top one?

_____

_____

_____

2. What did you learn from the diagram on page 7?

_____

_____

3. Why do you think the author included the diagrams on pages 8 and 9?

_____

_____

4. Sometimes the caption that goes with a picture tells something that the text does not. What do you learn from the caption on page 12 that is not in the text?

_____

_____

5. What does the graphic feature on page 18 show you?

_____

_____

Name _____

Vocabulary

Directions Choose the word from the box that means the same or nearly the same as the underlined part of each sentence. Write the word on the line.

Check the Words You Know

__astronauts	__capsule	__hatch	__horizon
__lunar	__module	__quarantine	

---

1. The Earth casts a shadow during an eclipse <u>of the moon</u> .

   _____

2. Three of the <u>crew members of the spacecraft</u> on the *Apollo 1* mission died because of a fire on board.

   _____

3. Astronauts returning to Earth after a mission are often kept in <u>isolation to prevent the spread of disease</u>.

   _____

4. *Vostok 1* was the first <u>front section of a rocket that carried people and supplies into space</u> to orbit Earth.

   _____

5. The moon rose above the <u>skyline</u>.

   _____

6. An astronaut on an early space walk had to be tied to the <u>self-contained unit within a larger system</u>.

   _____

7. The <u>door covering a spacecraft's opening</u> needs to be sealed tightly before a rocket is launched into space.

   _____

Directions Imagine that you are an astronaut visiting the moon. On a separate sheet of paper, write a story about your trip. Use at least three of the vocabulary words in your story.

_____

_____

Story Prediction from Previewing

Title _____

Read the title and look at the pictures in the story.
What do you think a problem in the story might be?

I think a problem might be _____

_____

_____

After reading _____ ,
draw a picture of one of the problems in the story.

Story Prediction from Vocabulary

Title _____

Look at the title above and the list of words and phrases below.
Write sentences that predict who and what this story might be about.

Words and Phrases

Characters: _____

_____

Problem: _____

_____

_____

_____

Events: _____

_____

_____

_____

Outcome: _____

_____

_____

_____

KWL Chart

Topic _____

What We **K**now	What We **W**ant to Know	What We **L**earned

Vocabulary Frame

Word

Association or Symbol

Predicted definition:

_____

_____

One good sentence:

_____

_____

_____

Verified definition:

_____

_____

Another good sentence:

_____

_____

_____

Story Sequence A

Title _____

Beginning

Middle

End

Story Sequence B

Title _____

Characters

Setting

Problem

Events

_____

_____

_____

_____

_____

_____

_____

_____

Solution

Story Elements

Title _____

This story is about _____

_____
(name the characters)

This story takes place _____

_____
(where and when)

The action begins when _____

_____

_____

Then, _____

_____

_____

Next, _____

_____

_____

After that, _____

_____

_____

The story ends when _____

_____

_____

Theme: _____

_____

Question the Author

Title _____

Author _____ **Page** _____

1. What does the author tell you?	
2. Why do you think the author tells you that?	
3. Does the author say it clearly?	
4. What would make it clearer?	
5. How would you say it instead?	

Plot Structure

Title _____

Characters _____

Setting _____

Climax
(Turning Point)

Rising Action

Solution
(Outcome)

Problem
(Goal)

Story Comparison

Characters

Characters

Setting

Setting

Events

Events

Ending

Ending

Web

Main Idea

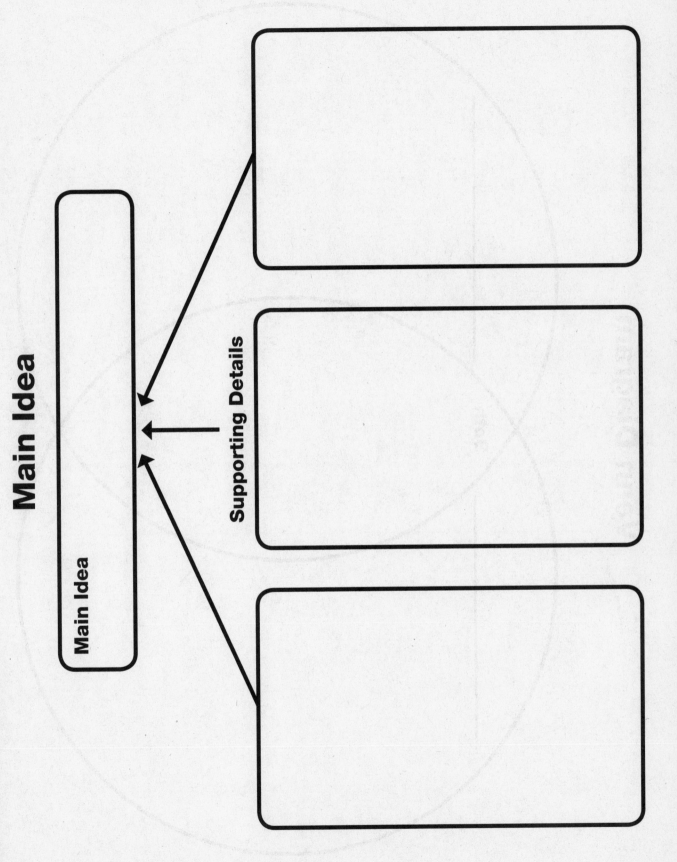

Main Idea

Supporting Details

Venn Diagram

Both

Compare and Contrast

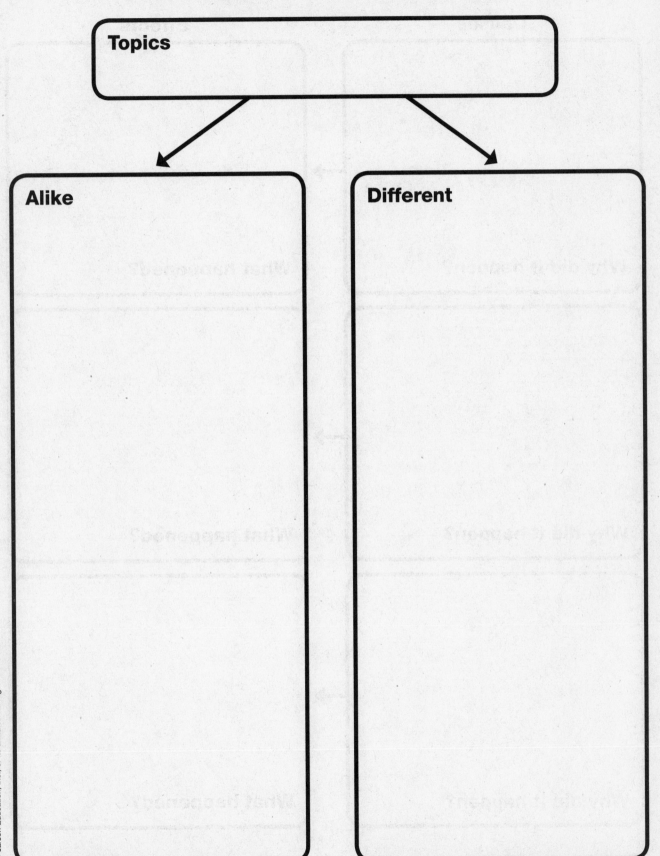

Topics

Alike

Different

Cause and Effect

Causes

Effects

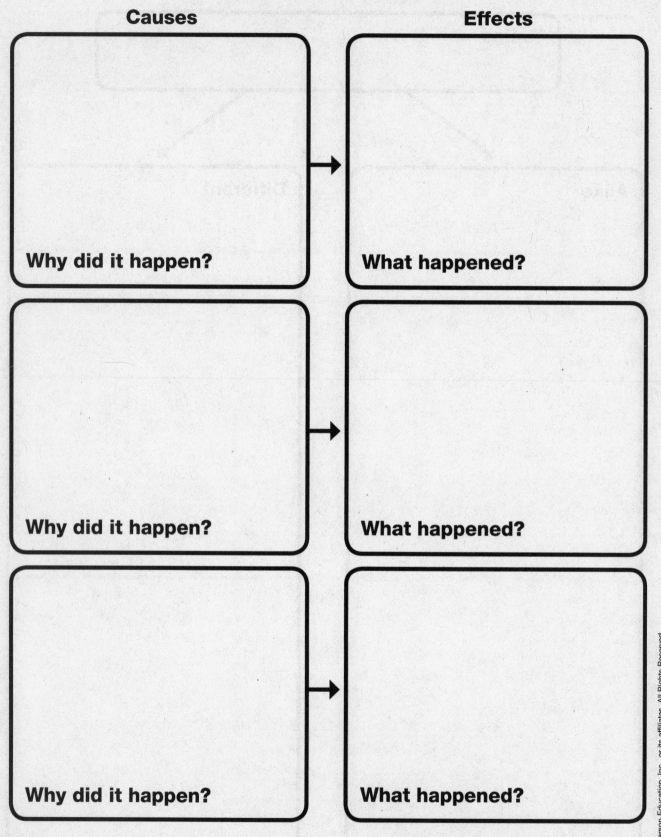

Why did it happen?

What happened?

Why did it happen?

What happened?

Why did it happen?

What happened?

Problem and Solution

Problem

Attempts to Solve the Problem

Solution

Time Line

Date

Steps in a Process

Process _____

```
┌─────────────────────────────────────────────┐
│ Step 1                                        │
│                                               │
│                                               │
└─────────────────────────────────────────────┘
                    ↓
┌─────────────────────────────────────────────┐
│ Step 2                                        │
│                                               │
│                                               │
└─────────────────────────────────────────────┘
                    ↓
┌─────────────────────────────────────────────┐
│ Step 3                                        │
│                                               │
│                                               │
└─────────────────────────────────────────────┘
                    ↓
┌─────────────────────────────────────────────┐
│ Step 4                                        │
│                                               │
│                                               │
└─────────────────────────────────────────────┘
                    ↓
┌─────────────────────────────────────────────┐
│ Step 5                                        │
│                                               │
│                                               │
└─────────────────────────────────────────────┘
```

Three-Column Chart

Four-Column Chart

Five-Column Chart

Answer Key

Leveled Reader Practice Pages

Florida Everglades: It's Plants & Animals p. 14
SEQUENCE
1. bear facts, bear trouble, bear food
2. many egrets were killed for their feathers. the feathers were used to decorate hats. the egret is protected.
3. many animals and plants lived in the Florida Everglades.
many animals and plants almost went extinct. the Florida Everglades is a protected habitat.
4. black bears, other animals, birds, plants, plants and animals together

Florida Everglades: It's Plants & Animals
p. 14 Vocabulary
1. positive
2. memorial
3. select
4. peculiar
5. grand
6. recall
7. prideful

Possible answers given.
8. ordinary, poor, small, minor
9. normal, ordinary, usual, common
10. ashamed, humble

The Long Journey West p. 18
AUTHOR'S PURPOSE
1. d
2. a
3. c
4. d

The Long Journey West p. 19 Vocabulary
1. docks
2. migrating
3. scan
4. yearned
5. wharf
6. scent
7. docks
8. scent
9. wharf
10. docks
11. migrating
12. scanned
13. yearned

From Sea to Shining Sea p. 22
CHARACTER, SETTING, AND PLOT
Possible responses given.
The story is about: Merriwether Lewis, William Clark, Corps of Discovery, Sacagawea, Tad, President Thomas Jefferson
This story takes place: Western part of the United States (rivers, plains, tribe reservation, fort, mountains, Pacific Ocean) between August 31, 1803 and fall 1806.
The action begins when: President Jefferson sends Lewis, Clark, and the Corps of Discovery to explore the West.
Then: Answers may vary but should include meeting the Yankton Sioux tribe.
Next: Answers may vary but should include that they built a fort to live in for the weekend.
After that: Answers may vary but should include that half of the group returns home to share discoveries with the President. The other half moves on.
The story ends when: Answers may vary but should include that the group reaches the Pacific Ocean and then return to share the remaining discoveries with the President.

From Sea to Shining Sea p. 23 Vocabulary
Sentences will vary.
1. ruffled
2. badger
3. rushes
4. bank
5. jointed
6. bristled
7. patched

Flash Flood p. 26
AUTHOR'S PURPOSE
1. a
2. c
3. d
4. b

Flash Flood p. 27 Vocabulary
1. c
2. e
3. d
4. a
5. b
6. f

Responses will vary. Students' stories or poems should use all three words correctly.

America's National Park p. 30
MAIN IDEA AND DETAILS
Possible responses provided.
1. Grand Canyon National Park is one of the most famous parks in the world.
2. Scientists come from all over the world to study the fossils in the canyon.
3. Other scientists come to study the wildlife.

4. Many tourists visit the park to admire it.

America's National Park p. 31 Vocabulary

1. b	6. impressive
2. e	7. species
3. c	8. preserve
4. a	9. slopes
5. d	10. wilderness

Cheers for the Cheetahs p. 34

CAUSE AND EFFECT

Possible answers given.

1. He thought boys were better at sports than girls because he always watched the boys and saw how good they were.
2. She wrote a letter.
3. The principal and the coach could get mad. The benefit was that they were able to prove themselves.
4. The coach will probably be more likely to give all girls a chance at sports now because he has seen that they can play well.
5. It is important to speak up for yourself. Hannah and her team did, and they got a chance to play that they would not have had otherwise.

Cheers for the Cheetahs p. 34 Vocabulary

1. h	8. a
2. b	9. fouled
3. d	10. hoop
4. g	11. jersey
5. c	12. rim
6. e	13. unbelievable
7. f	

Ranches in the Southwest p. 38

DRAW CONCLUSIONS

1. Cattle eat and trample plants. Cattle make waterways dirty. Cattle destroy plant growth, which threatens local plants and the animals that depend on them for food.
2. Guests learn how to rope cattle. They can take tennis or yoga. They are given comfortable quarters and good food.
3. Ranchers must be up before dawn; they aren't done until eight at night; ranching is still done in winter.
4. Answers will vary.

Ranches in the Southwest p. 39 Vocabulary

Underlined:
1. The coyote was bawling for its mother.
2. Wild coyotes live high in the mountains.

3. Sometimes they call guys "dudes."
4. At the roundup, all the cattle were put into pens.
5. The cowboy never used his spurs on his horses.

Sentences will vary.

What It Takes to Stage a Play p. 42

DRAW CONCLUSIONS

Possible responses:
1. Fact: The costume crew makes the costume.
2. Fact: Some crew members control the show's lighting.
3. Fact: The costumes help make the characters in the play look real.
4. Conclusion: are an important part of the play and help the play look believable.
5. Possible response: The props crew is important because they find the things that the actors use during the play.

What It Takes to Stage a Play p. 43

Vocabulary

1. dishonesty	6. arguments
2. advice	7. script
3. snag	8. not agree
4. descendant	9. not approve
5. arrangements	10. not like

Animal Helpers p. 46

FACT AND OPINION

1. Opinion	4. Opinion
2. Fact	5. Fact
3. Fact	6. Opinion

7. Responses will vary but should be examples of statements of fact.
8. Responses will vary but should be examples of statements of opinion.

Animal Helpers p. 47 Vocabulary

1. rickety
2. ambition
3. vast
4. landslide
5. infested
6. roamed
7. quicksand
8. resistance
9. Responses will vary, but sentences should include the correct use of the word *ambition*.
10. Responses will vary, but sentences should include the correct use of the word *rickety*.

A Trip to Capitol Hill p. 50
MAIN IDEA AND DETAILS
Possible response given.
1. The Founding Fathers wanted the United States to have a strong government.
2. In the Constitution, they outlined three branches of government.
3. The three branches are the legislative, executive, and judicial.
4. Each branch has different responsibilities; all branches are designed to help the government run smoothly.
5. Each branch has the power to challenge the others.

A Trip to Capitol Hill p. 51 Vocabulary
1. solemnly
2. Constitution
3. humble
4. politics
5. responsibility
6. howling
7. vain
Responses will vary.

Looking for Changes p. 54
GRAPHIC SOURCES
Possible responses:
1. The size of the ice covering the Arctic Ocean was smaller in 2003 than in 1979.
2. The average temperature of Earth has risen several degrees over the past 140 years.
3. Responses will vary but make sure students understand the concept of the greenhouse effect.
4. Responses may vary but make sure students understand the effects of the clouds of smoke coming out of the factory smokestacks.
5. parts of speech and definition

Looking for Changes p. 55
1. essay
2. apprentice
3. manufacturing
4. chemical
5. club
6. atmosphere
7. pressure
8. scales
Responses will vary.

The Gray Whale p. 58
FACT AND OPINION
Responses will vary.
Statements of Fact: Facts about what gray whales look like, what they eat, how and where they migrate, and how they communicate should be included.
Statements of Opinion: Opinions may include students' own as well as from the book: People enjoy touching a gray whale.
Responses will vary.

The Gray Whale p. 59
1. bluff
2. tropical
3. massive
4. biologists
5. lagoon
6. rumbling
7. lagoon
8. tropical
9. massive
10. rumbling
11. bluff
12. biologists
13–18. Responses will vary

Day for Night p. 62
GENERALIZE
Possible responses given.
1. By the end of the 1600s, most people believed that Earth moved around the sun.
2. Copernicus, Kepler, and Galileo were all confident and smart scientists.
3. They all agreed that Earth revolved around the sun.
4. They all worked to prove the theory.
5. They all tried to persuade others.

Day for Night p. 63 Vocabulary
1. d. radiant—giving off bright steady light
2. c. choir—a group of people who sing together
3. b. yellow-belly—someone who is afraid
4. e. beamed—shone light in one direction
5. a. twinkling—giving off flickering light
Possible responses given.
6. The brilliant star could be seen in the cloudy night sky.
7. Galileo was not a coward, since he stood up to powerful people.
8. Early this morning, sunlight gleamed through my window.
9. Looking at the shimmering stars makes me feel small.
10. The chorus sang many songs at the concert.

Surviving Hurricane Andrew p. 66
CAUSE AND EFFECT
1. Cause: The sand spit makes the wave smaller; Effect: it is safer for people to swim.
2. Cause: Scamp was barking; Effect: I picked him up and held him.
3. Cause: We used duct tape to put Xs on them; Effect: the windows didn't shatter.
4. Possible responses: the strong winds of Hurricane Andrew; the tree knocked it over
5. the fish stay fresh

Surviving Hurricane Andrew p. 67 Vocabulary
1. expected
2. forecasts
3. inland
4. shatter
5. surge
6. destruction

Answers will vary. Stories should be about hurricanes and correctly use all of the vocabulary words.

Saving Trees by Using Science p. 70
GENERALIZE
Responses in web will vary, but should reflect details in the passage.
Generalization: Rain forests will always play an important role in our world.

Saving Trees by Using Science p. 71
Vocabulary
1. requirements
2. harness
3. announcement
4. untamed
5. feature
6. lumberjacks
7. thaw
8. unnatural
9–10. Sentences will vary.

Mini Microbes p. 74
COMPARE AND CONTRAST
Possible responses:
Yeast: microbes feed on sugar; create gas bubbles; make dough rise; create tiny holes
Both: microbes; eat; reproduce; alter food; we see the changes
Mold: microbes come from air; feed on bread; cover the surface

Mini Microbes p. 75 Vocabulary
analysis: 5; beakers: 1; hollow: 2; identify: 8; lecture: 4; microscope: 6; precise: 3; relentless: 7
Students should locate all vocabulary words in the word search box.

Dolphins: Mammals of the Sea p. 78
COMPARE AND CONTRAST
1. All are mammals that bear live young: all are warm-blooded
2. Bottle-nosed dolphins have gray upper bodies with pinkish bellies. Hourglass dolphins have sharp black-and-white coloring.
3. Bottle-nosed dolphins' beaks are about 7cm long: hourglass dolphins have shorter beaks
4. Bottle-nosed dolphins are found in coastal waters, while hourglass dolphins are found in the cold waters off Antarctica.

Dolphins: Mammals of the Sea p. 79
1. enchanted
2. glimpses
3. aquarium
4. surface
5. pulses
6. dolphins
7. flexible
8. dolphins
9. surface
10. enchanted

Speaking in Code p. 82
SEQUENCE
4, 6, 3, 2, 1, 5
Responses will vary.

Speaking in Code p. 83 Vocabulary
1. d
2. f
3. g
4. b
5. h
6. e
7. a
8. c
9. intense—Sentences will vary.
10. messages—Sentences will vary.
11. advance—Sentences will vary.
12. impossible—Sentences will vary.

The Rosetta Stone: The Key to Ancient Writings p. 86
GRAPHIC FEATURES
1. Rosetta Stone made
2. Egypt becomes part of Roman Empire
3. Rosetta Stone found
4. Rosetta Stone displayed in The British Museum.
5–8. Time lines should show the events in chronological order and the events should be spaced to reflect the time span between them.

The Rosetta Stone: The Key to Ancient Writings p. 87 Vocabulary
Across:
2. triumph
3. cover
4. temple
5. scholars
7. link

Down:
1. ancient
2. translate
3. seeker

Top Hat Tompkins, The Detective p. 90
CHARACTER AND PLOT
Characters: Top Hat, Sid, Penny, Ralph, Hugh
Conflict: Sid's salamanders are missing.

5. Event 1: Top Hat and Sid talk to Penny Prundle.
9. Event 2: Top Hat and Sid talk to Ralph Moobly.
11. Event 3: Top Hat talks to Hugh and finds out that Hugh makes ice sculptures.
14. Event 4: Top Hat has one more question for Sid.
16. Climax: Top Hat returns with the salamander in a box.
17–19. Resolution: Top Hat explains how he solved the mystery.

Top Hat Tompkins, The Detective p. 91
Vocabulary
1. confused
2. amphibian
3. reptile
4. unlawful act
5. display
6. book of facts
7. reptiles
8. salamanders
9. amphibians
10. stumped

Putting a Stop to Wildfires p. 94
AUTHOR'S PURPOSE
Possible responses given.
1. The author's main purpose for writing is to inform people about wildfires, how they start, and the people who put them out.
2. to inform the reader of another type of firefighter
3. to show the equipment that hotshots need.
4. It could be changed into a fictional story about firefighters that entertains readers.

Putting a Stop to Wildfires p. 95 Vocabulary
1. essential
2. dedication
3. parachute
4. concentrating
5. wind
6. methods
7. underbrush
8. steer
Responses will vary.

Let's Get to Know the Incas p. 98
COMPARE AND CONTRAST
1. unlike
2. in contrast
3. same
4. however
5. like
6. but
7. Unlike
8. in contrast
9. but
10. similar to

Let's Get to Know the Incas p. 99 Vocabulary
1. thickets
2. granite
3. curiosity
4. torrent
5. glorious
6. granite
7. ruins
8. terraced
9. curiosity
10. granite
11. ruins
12. thickets
13. torrent
14. glorious
15. terraced

Mountain Rescue p. 102
SETTING AND PLOT
Possible response:
1. Title: Mountain Rescue
2. Marisa, her brother Alvaro, and Abuela, their grandmother.
3. in Grand Teton National Park
4. Marisa and Al go for a hike after Marisa has an argument with Abuela.
5. Marisa and Al find a lamb trapped on a ledge.
6. Al hurts his arm while rescuing the lamb.
7. Al and Marisa head for home with Marisa carrying the lamb on her shoulders.
8. Abuela meets Al and Marisa with her flashlight and guides them safely home.

Mountain Rescue p. 103 Vocabulary
1. rappel
2. void
3. coil
4. descent
5. trekked
6. foresaw
7. shaft
8. ridge
9. coil
10. descent
11. rappel
12. foresaw

Plants and Animals in Antarctica p. 106
MAIN IDEA AND DETAILS
1. Antarctica's climate
2. Antarctica is a cold, harsh place.
3–5. Winter is long, dark, and cold.
Blizzards can blow snow at 100 miles an hour.
Blizzards can last a long time.

Plants and Animals in Antarctica
p. 107 Vocabulary
1. e
2. a
3. c
4. d
5. b
6–10. Sentences will vary.

Stuart's Moon Suit p. 110
DRAW CONCLUSIONS
Students should include the information they learned in the book about each component of the space suit.
Student responses will vary. They should include facts from the book to back up their answers.

Stuart's Moon Suit p. 111 Vocabulary
1. rile
2. loomed
3. trudged
4. taunted
5. runt
6. staggered
7. trench
8. summoning
9. trudged
10. summoning
11. runt
12. loomed
13. trench
14. staggered
15. rile
16. taunted

We Shall Overcome p. 114
CAUSE AND EFFECT
Possible responses given.
2. William Lloyd Garrison publishes *The Liberator*.
3. Frederick Douglass speaks about equality.
4. Sojourner Truth travels to speak out about ending slavery.
5. The Abolitionist Movement spread the word of freedom. It drew attention to the suffering slaves. As a result, the Emancipation Proclamation was signed in 1863 which freed enslaved people in the Confederate states in rebellion.

We Shall Overcome p. 115 Vocabulary
1. f
2. e
3. d
4. a
5. b
6. c
7. generations
8. shielding
9. avoided
10. minister

The Sauk and Fox: Native Americans p. 118
FACT AND OPINION
1–8. Answers will vary.

The Sauk and Fox: Native Americans p. 119 Vocabulary
1. reservation
2. boarding schools
3. dormitory
4. manual
5. endurance
6. society
Answers will vary.

Living with Grandpa Joseph p. 122
SEQUENCE
1. 4
2. 6
3. 1
4. 9
5. 5
6. 7
7. 2
8. 10
9. 3
10. 8

Living with Grandpa Joseph p. 123
1. resemblance
2. colonel
3. glint
4. affords
5. palette
6. quaint
7. lurking
Responses will vary.

To Be a Star p. 126
GENERALIZE
Possible responses: Becky thought about what he said before she fell asleep; Becky decided to switch parts with Marta; Becky was nervous before the play began but then her grandpa's advice made her relax; Becky was happy after the play ended because she had followed her grandpa's advice.

To Be a Star p. 127 Vocabulary
1. ceremonial
2. graze
3. shock
4. abundance
5. drought
6. backdrop
7–9. Sentences will vary.

Earth's Closest Neighbor p. 130
GRAPHIC FEATURES
Possible answers given.
1. I know how big a tennis ball and a basketball are, so I can see just how much smaller the moon is compared to Earth.
2. the names and shapes of the different phases of the moon; how the moon goes through different phases as it orbits Earth.
3. to help me understand how solar and lunar eclipses work
4. *The Saturn V* rocket was made to send a crew to the moon.
5. the parts of the spacecraft; the Service Module and the Command Module

Earth's Closest Neighbor p. 131 Vocabulary
1. lunar
2. astronauts
3. quarantine
4. capsule
5. horizon
6. module
7. hatch
8. Responses will vary.